LIBRARY
SOUTHERN CENTER/GGBTS

The HARD SAYINGS of JESUS

The HARD SAYINGS of JESUS

Albert McClellan

Broadman Press
Nashville, Tennessee

© Copyright 1975 · BROADMAN PRESS
All rights reserved
4213-40
ISBN: 0-8054-1340-5

232.95
.M13

All Scripture quotations marked (TEV) are from *Today's English Version* © American Bible Society 1966, 1970, 1971 and are used by permission.

Subject Heading: Jesus Christ—Teaching
Dewey Decimal Classification: 232.954
Library of Congress Catalog Card Number: 73-83827
Printed in the United States of America

For
Renick Helm and Alan Brownlow

Contents

1. A Hard Way to Go 11
2. The Heavy Burden That Is Light 18
3. Final Freedom 24
4. King on a Donkey 30
5. Appearances Are Secondary 35
6. When Confession Rings True 44
7. Man's Ultimate Failure 51
8. Treasures of the Heart 58
9. Let the Dead Alone 65
10. Harlots First 74
11. The Holy Option 79
12. The Firebringer 86
13. The Hardest Truth 91
14. The Making of a Fool 97
15. Knowing God 101
16. "I Call You Friends" 107
17. With Everything 114
18. The Hardest Commandment 122
19. Becoming Perfect 126
    Notes 134

Introduction

After a long dispute with the people in which Jesus said, "I am the bread of life" (John 6:35, RSV), and "He who eats me will live because of me" (John 6:57, RSV), many of his disciples said in amazement, "This is a hard saying: who can listen to it?" (John 6:60, RSV). They were overcome by the revolutionary ideas and extreme requirements of the gospel, and they found the words of Jesus hard to understand, hard to accept, and hard to follow. Their reaction was not very much different from the reaction of the world today.

Familiarity with the sayings of Jesus lead men either to overlook their stringency and their austerity, or to regard them too romantically or too wishfully. They do not always realize that at the bottom of every one are meanings that can change haters into lovers, keepers into givers, fools into sages, and losers into winners. Even if they understand their radical meanings, they find it difficult to surrender to their radical demands.

This book is an effort to bring to light the hard meanings of nineteen of the sayings of Jesus, and to give them dimension in terms of the new times in which we live. It is the author's conviction that they are as startling and true in today's world as they were 2,000 years ago when they were spoken. To believe them is to live, and to ignore them is to die. This claim is astonishing to some, as it was to the crowds who first Jesus spoke his words (Matt. 7:28), yet the truth abides: "Every one then who hears these words of mine and does them will be like a wise man who built his house upon the rock; and the rain fell, and the floods came, and the winds blew and beat upon that house, but it did not fall, because it had been founded on the rock. And everyone who hears these words of mine and does not do them will be like a foolish man who built his house upon the sand; and the rain fell, and the floods came, and the winds blew and beat against that house, and it fell; and great was the fall of it" (Matt. 7:24-27).

ALBERT MCCLELLAN

1
A Hard Way to Go

"Go in through the narrow gate, for the gate is wide and the road is easy that leads to hell, and there are many who travel it. The gate is narrow and the way is hard that leads to life, and few people find it" (Matt. 7:13-14, TEV).

Herschel H. Hobbs said that "life" as used in this text means "abundance of living which should be the experience of every Christian."[1] John A. Broadus described it as "spiritual and eternal life."[2] Charles J. Ellicott said that it summed up "all the blessedness of the Kingdom."[3] The ancient Chrysostom thought it meant the heavenly city.[4] Matthew Henry called it a "state of grace."[5]

All of these mean about the same thing.

Life in the eternal sense is what Jesus Christ gives of himself as man moves toward him. It is a special reality, a personal fulfillment, a quality of individual being that comes, not from our own achievements, but from our surrender to him. Most men seek only life, when it is Life they need. They never know the true shape of their deep yearnings. They thirst, not knowing that life in Christ is water for their thirst. They hunger, not knowing that the life in Christ is bread for their hunger. They want life. Many fail to find it, but some do find it.

Everyone wants life. They seek it both passionately and blindly. Perhaps even the people who take their own lives want life, not what they have but something else. Not finding it, they kill themselves. The woman who met Jesus at the well appeared to be despairing of life. When Jesus told her of the water of everlasting life which would quench her deep thirst, she eagerly asked for it. The very possibility of the waters awakened in her the hope for an answer to her deep inner need. She had lived so long in sin, thinking that sin was life, that she had totally missed the meaning of life. Like so many others she wanted life, yet she had not known what it was. The words of Jesus helped her to see that life could be triumphant.

Most people, including the young and the old, settle for a limited earthbound life. They see it as something physically hemmed in by time and memory; they do not realize that true life is spiritual and eternal and that it extends both backward beyond their memory and forward beyond their expectations—to something which they do not yet see, but something in which they can participate forever. In other words, they know life in themselves but not in God; they are not truly "turned on" to the eternal.

This phrase "turned on" is a curious one, invented in our time to describe people meeting life in a bold, physical, imaginative way. If one sees possibilities another does not see, he is "turned on." If one responds with enthusiasm, he is said to be "turned on." If one is physically uninhibited, he is "turned on." Such living requires faith and courage, and it is the better way. The "turned off" way is to be doubtful and fearful, and to take hold of life as if it were a soiled handkerchief in the gutter. Optimistic and aggressive "turning on" is certainly not evil within itself.

However, this is not what many modern young people mean by "turning on." Their idea of life turns toward evil.

A HARD WAY TO GO

Some throw marriage overboard and cohabit indiscriminately. Some abandon work as a worthy pursuit. Others turn against the morés and moralities of their parents, or they flout the church. A few parade naked in the streets. Such are said to be "turned on." This suggests the dilemma of most people, young and old—they look for life and find only death. They want life, but they miss it.

Many people miss out on life. This is best illustrated by what happens with the use of the hallucinogenic drugs such as mescaline or LSD. The mind turns inside out, the subconscious and the unconscious become hyperactive, the human organism goes wild, and all kinds of visual fantasies replace reality. This is strictly a physical or sensate "turning on," yet some people have called it spiritual. It can lead to total dysfunction of the body and the personality and to a cop-out on duty and responsibility. It can lead to death with the users dreaming that they can fly off the top of buildings or stop cars on the highway.

Similar things may be said of alcohol. Such "turning on" is false and evasive. It occurs more often than not because the victim cannot or will not face the hard ultimate questions of sin, law, death, and judgment.

There is another kind of "turning on" that can be just as bad, though it may also be good. It is the broad way of culture and things. By "culture" we mean such things as intellectual and artistic activity, a style or social grace, the products of human work and thought, accepted behavioral traditions, the standards in art and literature set by the informed people, or a particular level of attainment of civilization. By "things" we mean: possessions, belonging, objects of both extrinsic and intrinsic worth, houses, cars, stocks and bonds, silver pieces, art objects, jewelry, clothing, books, and any other material possessions that can be handled, tasted, smelled or felt, seen or hidden, or idolized.

Jesus did not condemn culture or things. In his ministry he honored men of learning and of wealth, and at the end of his life he permitted an alabaster bottle of perfume to be spilled on his head. What he did condemn was a mean, narrow worship of culture and things as if they equated life. He told of a man who kept building bigger barns to hold his crops only to lose his own soul. He warned that it is easier for a camel to go through a needle eye than for a rich man to enter the kingdom of God. Jesus wanted both culture and things to be used in the right ways, the sure wrong way being as a substitute for the Life which he gives.

Life in Jesus Christ is life of the highest reality, the life of the Spirit. It comes not from the externals of personality but from a deep moving of man and God toward a meeting of each other at the end of repentance, where faith becomes real, and where God and man are joined as one in Christ. In short, it comes from the depths and riches of the spiritual life when the self chooses God.

Long ago in a German refugee camp I saw women from an iron-curtain country clinging to their little bundles of possessions. One of these was opened to me. It was filled with broken bottles, pieces of worn faded cloth, sticks, tin cans, bent nails, old clothing. The whole bundle was not worth even 15 cents, but these women would fight over these bundles. In that same camp, I heard three refugee teenagers singing, "This Is My Father's World." William Barclay in his study of this passage said that there are two ways for man: "the high way" and "the low." He quoted John Oxenham, "The high soul treads the high way, and the low soul gropes the low." [6] One could hope that the singing teenagers had really chosen the high, narrow way. It is so much better than the bundle of trash called life which most people shape for themselves.

Some people do find life. We must examine a little more closely that "narrow" way. Why is the way narrow and why does it become more narrow? The individual, when at last he comes to himself, finds that he is covered with layers and layers of pretensions, illusions, traditions, and false ideas. He is scarcely himself at all. He is indeed part of all that he has ever met, or at least all is part of himself: He is not himself, not the naked soul before God.

The gate where God has planned to meet him is as narrow as the cross, and there is room there only for man in Christ in God. If man truly repents, if he turns around and faces that narrow gate, and if he pursues it, he will find the closer he gets to it that all his false layers keep bumping the narrow sides. He will strip as he runs, throwing away his pride, his pretension, his false ideas, his dependence on things, his empty traditions until at last he comes to the gate clean and whole before God. Along the way he moves from the physical world to the spiritual world, from the temporal world to the eternal world, from the world of self alone to the world of self in God.

The last piece of baggage that the person moving toward Christ throws away is the mirror in which he sees himself alone. In its place he sees himself in God. In the Christian sense, he has moved from the world of unreality into the world of reality. All things are put in their places. The joy he once found in things he now finds in spirit. From now on he is in Christ, and he is free. He becomes truly "turned on." He has found his spring for action, and he becomes spiritually aware. God blesses him with a new creative spirit.

The way may be hard and narrow, and the gate also narrow, but beyond it, all the world and heaven are his. "For all things are yours; whether Paul, or Apollos, or Cephas, or the world, or life, or death, or things present, or things to come; all are yours" (1 Cor. 3:21-22). The narrow way gives way to the broadest way of all, life in Christ. "Ye are Christ's and Christ is God's" (1 Cor. 3:23). Literally, in Christ, in his Spirit, the person has become a new creature, the greatest mark of which is freedom. He has obtained "the glorious liberty of the children of God" (Rom. 8:21, RSV).

In his new life he is free from the bondage of sin because God's grace is available to him. He is available to him. He is free from the bondage of self-justification because Christ now is his justification. He is free from the law because he does not now live by the law but by the Spirit. He is free from the sting of death because Christ has given him life that reaches beyond death. He is free from meaningless traditions because Christ alone has become his truth. All of the questions of sin, law, death, and judgment have not been solved, but they have been committed to an Advocate who will solve them for him. This new life is not a "do as you like" freedom, rather it is freedom as servants of others because of the law of love; its highest expression is living for others.

One more thing: the idea that life lies ahead, beyond the narrow gate leads to one final observation about this text—that life must be lived forward. We live the Life only after we are in it. We understand it by looking back to the moment when we threw overboard all of our useless baggage and stood whole and bare in Christ in God. Youth who realize this abandonment will find a glorious life full of surprises, and the aged who realize it will know surely that in his life the best is yet to be. But failing to realize it, both youth and aged have only one thing to look forward to—destruction.

2
The Heavy Burden That Is Light

"Come to me, all of you who are tired from carrying your heavy loads, and I will give you rest" (Matt. 11:28, TEV).

Earl Waldrup is my friend, an ordinary man with ordinary talents, and yet a man different from most men. His difference is this—his Christianity shows in his smile and his manner. He is not gushy or vain, and he does not overflow with excessive religious talk. He does, however, overflow with faith, and his faith is contagious.

In a talk to our church, he said that the last five years had brought him into deeper awareness of what it means to be a Christian. The way he said it made it seem that he had just found out about it. Yet I remember hearing him say about the same thing twenty years ago. You see, Earl has always been moving into a deeper awareness of what it means to be a Christian. His walk with the Lord has been a pilgrimage into spiritual purity.

This does not mean that Earl is perfect or that he is outwardly different from other men. It does mean that deep inside his life he has given Jesus Christ a greater place of continuity, intensity, and reality. Without fear and without reservation, he has buried his own spirit in the spirit of Christ.

When I say that he is an ordinary man, I mean that he does the things other men do, like mowing grass, washing the car, painting gutters, forming a car pool, and going to his office. These are the material zones of his life, but he enters into them spiritually; and gradually the Spirit is replacing for him all earthly sustenance, not by eliminating it but by transforming it. This is what shows on his countenance when he stands before the church and his special ray of spiritual sunshine illuminates the congregation.

In his talk he said he had learned three things: (1) God is always with him in the Holy Spirit. (2) God wants desperately to help him. (3) God is willing to answer his prayers. Earl has come to that marvelous moment of spiritual awareness when he accepts literally and trustingly the words of Jesus, "Come to me, all of you who are tired from carrying your heavy loads, and I will give you rest. Take my yoke and put it on you, and learn from me, because I am gentle and humble in spirit; and you will find rest. The yoke I will give you is easy, and the load I will put on you is light" (Matt. 11:28-30, TEV). Like countless other Christians, Earl has found that the Christian way is the happiest way, a truth the world does not want to accept. It prefers to believe that the yoke of Christ is hard and his load heavy.

To understand this we need to look at the people Jesus was addressing and examine the heavy loads they carried. The "heavy loads" were the works of the law, and the people before him were the scribes and the Pharisees, men who made their religion a material and outward adornment. They had striven for a righteousness of works not of faith; like oxen, their laws and their creeds, their traditions and their ceremonies had become yokes of dead, scalding weight. They were stumbling and falling under oppression greater than they could bear.

Jesus saw himself as the gentle master, the ox driver who loves and protects his oxen. He threw away creeds and traditions, and he humanized law. He cried out with pity for the bleeding backs of the Pharisees: "The yoke I give you is easy, and the load I put on you is light." This is his cry for all humanity, whatever their burdens and their sufferings.

In thinking about his words, we must not ourselves take the yoke of the law too literally. It means far more than rules and ceremonies. It extends into every dimension of human relationship and symbolizes the vast array of inhumanities that men inflict on one another. A religion of law sets men cruelly against their brothers. It categorizes and classifies people into tight pigeonholes, and it refuses to recognize that all are indeed of one flesh and one blood. It creates divisions and fightings, envies and jealousies, greed and murder. The religion of law does not trust man or honor man or believe that man can become better. It destroys man by smothering him in an artificial person that sometimes smells of wax and incense but more often of tar and feathers.

The heaviest burdens that most men bear is the heavy weight of political, social, and economic systems that seem to want to destroy them as an individual, robbing them of their inner dignity and manhood.

The alternative way is the way of faith, the entrance into a spiritual sphere where the humble spirit is king and where men love their brothers. Jesus is that King, and he invites all men to join him in his kingdom. "Come to me," he said, "learn of me. The yoke I give is easy, and the load I will put upon you is light." What does it mean to come to Jesus and to learn of him?

To come to Jesus we must listen to him. At the very bottom of life, where failure is ever present, where regrets and recriminations seize us, where dreams lie broken, and where all hope is gone, man can face only two ways. Set before him are two exactly opposite choices, a crushing and inexorable "either-or." *Either* he faces away from God viewing the wreck of his own life and moving forever in its morass, *or* he faces toward God away from his personal tragedy and begins to move toward the joy and the victory that God has promised in his kingdom of humility.

The turning is the thing, and it is the plan of God that Jesus Christ gives the power to turn. As a man in history, Jesus walks with him, an elder brother who knew a bitterness deeper than his own, a helper who becomes strength for him. Jesus speaks to him in his misery and calls his name and says, "Come to me." To heed that call is to be given a name, an identification, a personhood. It is to accept the truth that one is real in God. It is the first step toward spiritual purity, a cleansing of the past, a renewal of self, and the promise of hope. Man turns to find that in facing Christ he is facing God.

To listen to Jesus is to learn of him. When I say that my friend Earl Waldrup has buried his spirit in the spirit of Christ, I mean that he is dominated day and night in the physical, material world in which he must live—the world of hammering and digging, picnicking and writing, speaking and counseling—by a deep inner desire to give the spirit of Jesus Christ supreme place in his life. What is that spirit? In short, meekness and lowliness; in long, it is "whatever is true, whatever is honorable, whatever is just, whatever is pure, whatever is lovely, whatever is gracious" (Phil. 4:8, RSV). It is the opposite of being shut in to oneself or of living solely for one's own pleasure, wholly within oneself and around oneself. It is the opposite of whatever closes one's mind and heart to other people.

We listen by reading the words of Jesus and immersing ourselves in the details of his life. We listen by calling his name and speaking to him of our deepest needs. We listen by simply being quiet in his presence. We find that listening works miracles, for soon we learn that the One we are listening to is inside ourselves.

To learn of Jesus is to find him inside ourselves. When Jesus addresses a man, he is asking him to take him home with him, and the home he has in mind is the soul of the self of the man. This is one of the most beautiful realities of the gospel. In surrendering to him, man finds that Christ comes to live at the very center of his life. This means that where man most needs to look for Christ is deep within himself.

The psychologists say that the mind of man is composed of two parts, the conscious and the unconscious and that his actions are determined by both. They also say that the conscious is only the tip of the iceberg and that the unconscious has by far the greater influence. Whether this is theory or fact, we can only guess. But suppose it is true, and that there is a vast impenetrable realm of reality that is manifestly you, and that it has direct bearing on all that you consciously say and do.

What does this imply for the Christian? First, it means that he must open the darkest and most hidden recesses of his life to Christ, the unknown as well as the known. He must let Christ enter to cleanse and to redeem that part of his life that he cannot see or remember. Second, it means that the Christian has a marvelous power for living and being. The psychologists have a great deal to say about the power of the unconscious in ordinary men. But for the extraordinary person, the Christian, if Christ comes

THE HEAVEN BURDEN THAT IS LIGHT

to live in his already powerful unconscious, think what this means in the help he has for dealing with the problems of life. And third, it implies that each one of us must search for Christ in the deep unconscious areas of our lives. We must learn to probe the depths and to give our Lord access to the remote unknown of our inner selves.

One of the great experiences we can have is to enter actively into our own unconscious. It is dangerous, and without faith it can lead to disaster; but with faith it can lead to unparalleled freedom. We go deeper and deeper into ourselves, past all the facades and personas of false being, past the myths and fairy tales we create about ourselves, beyond the layers and layers of sin and pride, deeper still into the great cavern of the soul, down to the quivering reality, and there as he promised, if we live by faith, we find Jesus Christ, the maker and shaper of our unconscious, the great light of our lives, hidden though revealed and at the end of everything. There we make our greatest confession. "It is Jesus Christ within us, else we are failures." (Compare 2 Cor. 13:5, Moffatt.) We become real because he makes us real, giving us true liberty. We find in him a yoke that is easy and a burden that is light. It is then that we can rise up with wings as an eagle and soar to the stars.

And yet the world does not believe this. They find simple sayings of Jesus too hard to understand and too hard to follow. They much prefer their heavy yokes and impossible burdens.

3
Final Freedom

> So Jesus said to the Jews who believed in him, "If you obey my teaching you are really my disciples; you will know the truth, and the truth will make you free."
> "We are the descendants of Abraham," they answered, "and we have never been anybody's slaves. What do you mean, then, by saying, 'You will be free'?"
> Jesus said to them: "I tell you the truth: everyone who is is a slave of sin. A slave does not belong to the family always: but a son belongs there for ever. If the Son makes you free, then you will be really free" (John 8:31-36, TEV).

Freedom is what man most reaches for all of his life. Even on his natal day he will fight his dress, his blanket, or even his umbilical cloth if it binds him too tightly. Later he will climb out of his crib and maybe out of the window. He will run up the street to see what he has not seen before. As he gets older, he will fight to peel his own bananas and to choose his own clothing. His life struggle is always toward freedom.

Sometimes he finds freedom, sometimes he does not. Far too often, he has the misfortune of following the illusion of freedom. What often seems to him to be freedom turns out to be only a new slavery. For example, a young woman will say, "I'm free, so I choose drugs." Soon she is caught in a terrible habit to which her whole life is sacrificed. She never knows what true freedom means either at the beginning of her life or at the end.

FINAL FREEDOM

Freedom, of course, is a very complex thing. Dietrich Von Hildebrand said that there are two spheres of freedom.[1] The first is the innate freedom of man and he identifies it as having two dimensions. The first is one's right to say a yes or a no to a situation. The other dimension is one's capacity to enact decrees or commands within his range of effectiveness. The second sphere of freedom is moral or spiritual freedom. This is an endowment and the highest freedom possible.

Innate freedom comes to a man because he is a man. Endowed freedom comes to man as a child of God. The first is temporal, the second is eternal. The first is more or less protected by law, the second is guaranteed by grace. St. Augustine wrote of the two freedoms. He called them "minor liberty" and "major liberty."[2]

Nicolai Berdyaev, a twentieth-century Christian philosopher, described three freedoms.[3] The first is "primordial, irrational freedom which precedes good and evil and determines choice between them," and the second is "final, reasonable freedom, freedom in good and truth." The first is the freedom man is born with, and the second is the freedom toward which he moves all of his life. The third freedom is freedom in Christ which comprehends the other two. "The truth of Christ, which makes us free, does not force or compel anyone: it is not like the truths of this world which forcibly organize spirit and deprive it of freedom."

Most men fight desperately to achieve and preserve the lesser freedoms, the ones that Augustine called "minor," Hildebrand called "innate," and Berdyaev called "primordial." Few push on to find the greatest freedom of the Spirit, the freedom that lifts them above the world and makes them a child of eternity. They are willing to settle for a kind of *spirit of freedom,* but they find it difficult to go to the higher reaches of *freedom of the spirit.* In the first place, they do not understand freedom except as the opposite of authority and law; and in the second place, they are not willing to accept God's terms for the possessing of the freedom of the spirit.

They resist God at two points. First, they reject the saying of Jesus, "If you obey my teaching . . . you will know the truth, and the truth will make you free" (John 8:31-32, TEV). This means they reject the place that revelation has in freedom. Second, they reject his other great saying on freedom, "If the Son makes you free, then you will be really free" (John 8:36, TEV). This means they reject Jesus Christ as the ultimate giver of freedom. They do not accept revelation and Christ as reality. For them, such acceptance requires an incredulous faith which they cannot give. Like the disciples who grumbled against some of the sayings of Jesus, they say, "This teaching is too hard. Who can listen to this?" (John 6:60, TEV).

If you obey my teaching . . . you will know the truth. Many sincere people quote only part of this verse and miss the meaning. They say, "You will know the truth, and the truth will make you free." Sometimes they go so far as to carve these words on the stone walls of secular libraries. They claim that the truth which frees is the reality of a thing or a situation, like two plus two make four or that water is made up of two parts hydrogen and one part oxygen. Such truth does indeed bring freedom but not ultimate freedom. Only the truth that centers in God's only Son can do that. This is the great news that Christ is in God reconciling the world unto himself. Jesus Christ himself as "the truth" climaxes the things he taught.

His sayings are not to be treated as magic charms to

FINAL FREEDOM

be put in silver boxes and hung on chains around the neck but as living instruments of freedom to be taken into the heart. Jesus was no early-day Mao flaunting a little red book of magic. His sayings are the truth about life, but more than this they are the truth of himself. He was God's Word to man who spoke God's words to man. Obedience of these words is the way to truth. Those who refuse to obey them will be like "a foolish man who built his house on the sand. The rain poured down, . . . and it fell" (Matt. 7:26-27, TEV). By rejecting the Word, not only does a man lose freedom, he loses himself, and that is a terrible loss.

The truth will make you free. It is far better to live by truth than by error. If one believes that two plus two equal five, he is in constant trouble, enough to destroy his happiness and his usefulness.

Search for truth, wherever it is to be found, is a praiseworthy undertaking. The world cannot do without its scientists and its scholars. These men grasp at shadows and straws to discover the true nature of things. What most of them do not see is that when they have built their largest telescope and look farthest into space, and when they have built their strongest microscope and looked deepest into human life that there, ultimately, at the end of all their looking, if indeed they find truth, they will find Jesus Christ as the true nature of things. "For all things were created by him, and all things exist through him and for him" (Rom. 11:36, TEV). He alone is truth, final truth, highest truth, absolute truth, ultimate truth.

The truth of Christ is boundless truth that comes to us as God's own freedom. It is not the freedom of man's limited sphere but the freedom of God's unlimited kingdom. It comes as an endowment of his grace and his glory, not merely a system to be written or spoken, but a Power to be lived.

Ours is an age of ceaseless restlessness. Men and women hunger for food they cannot find, thirst for water that they can only dream about, and yearn for reality that seems to be a fiction. In this search, they change jobs and careers, and they change mates and names. They travel, only to want to go home. They go home, only to want to leave again. They create noise and illusion—all in the search of something, they cannot name it. For them there is no felicity in career or family or fortune or friends or work. Why? Because deep within they want true freedom, and true freedom is never to be found in things. It is to be found only in God who has spoken to man in Christ. The true happiness which men seek in lesser truths they find only in the ultimate truth of Christ.

"If the Son makes you free, then you will be really free." The ultimate slavery is not ignorance but sin. Freedom that does not liberate from sin is not true freedom. The Pharisees were pleading a freedom based on ancestry. "We be Abraham's seed, and were never in bondage to any man" (John 8:33). This is like saying, "I'm a scientist; I am free." "I am Bohemian; I am free." "I am a hippy; I'm free." Jesus' answer to this is, "Every one who commits sin is a slave to sin" (John 8:34, RSV). The name you bear, your lineage, your affiliations, your social groups, your citizenship do not buy true liberty—if you sin, you are not free.

Put a man in chains, take away his citizenship, rob him of his right to work, put him in bondage to another man; these are not the worst slaveries. The worst is that man himself is not free inside himself. He carries resentment and defensiveness; he is envious and greedy, and he is cynical and mistrusting. He is aggressive, projecting, immoral, and uncaring. In short, he is a sinner and a slave. Even without chains and bondage, he is not a free man. Being a slave, he is like a man without a family. Perhaps this is at the bottom of much of the restlessness of our times; man has alienated himself through his sins from the human family. He is alone in the world and misguided and empty.

Jesus responds to his emptiness by saying that a son belongs to the family forever, and then in a marvelous play on words, "If the Son makes you free, then you will be really free." The Son makes slaves into sons. The freedom he gives is the same freedom he possesses. It is the fullness of God that comes to those who remain in his teaching and come to him as the truth. This is freedom indeed—the fullness of God.

Truly it is "for freedom Christ has set us free" (Gal. 5:1, RSV). Freedom from the law, from the curse of the law, from the yoke of ritual, from fear of death and sin.

A man I once knew would look pensively out into space. I would ask, "What are you thinking?" His answer, "I'm just thinking." Another time I might frame the question, "What are you looking for?" or, "What are you dreaming?" Again, he would say, "I'm just looking," or "I'm just dreaming." This symbolizes the quest of man for satisfaction he has not yet found. He thinks and does not understand; he dreams and does not discover; he looks and does not see. Bound, he cannot articulate his own slavery. When I see such men, their lives vastly different from what they had hoped they would be, I want to cry out to them: "Oh, my friend, come on to freedom. Come on to Christ. He is the one for whom you are looking and dreaming and thinking, and you know it not."

4
King on a Donkey

"You will find a donkey tied up and her colt with her . . . bring them to me" (Matt. 21:2, TEV).

A governor of a state pushed through a legislative bill to buy an $800,000 jet airplane. His argument was, "The people expect me to go first class." This seems to be a prevailing world view, "Go first class. If you don't, you'll leave the wrong image. People will think you are second class." So the mad race goes on. People buy cars they can't afford, homes they can't pay for, clothing beyond their means, and high-priced cuts of meat when other cuts would do just as well. Some of them even leave their families mortgaged because of their need for a first-class funeral. Worse than anything else they do, they merely pretend to be something more than they are. Their lives are long weary charades. Not generous, they try to be generous; not kind, they try to be kind.

What they don't realize is that a butterfly does not have to "try" to be a butterfly, or a rose does not have to "try" to be a rose. Such people accumulate all kinds of badges, none of them really harmful, but all of them pretending facades to disguise their own inner reality. They have less and less power and finally life falls in for them. Yet such people go on saying, "First class, that's my style. That's the way I am." Yet when they say it, they feel the hollow-

KING ON A DONKEY

ness of their own lives and keep reaching for more first-class honors. Like a narcotic, it takes more and more to satisfy.

The plain truth is that in a world of unequal opportunity everyone cannot go first class. The way life falls out, most people must go second class. This poses a sharp question, "If I can't go first class, does that make me a second-class human being?"

The world answers, "Yes."

Jesus answers, "No."

To prove his point Jesus sent for a donkey, a lowly ass, an onager, the braying long-eared animal that has been the onus of truth and fiction since the world began. He said, "Go to a certain place and there you will find a donkey. Bring them to me. If any object, say that your master has need of them."

Here the King is sending for a donkey. He wants to ride her in his coronation march. No white stallion, no golden chariot, no velvet-lined litter borne by men, just a common ass for a king to ride to his crowning. The world finds this hard to take. If only he had left unsaid, "Bring me a donkey," then the whole Christian life would be different. People want their kings to keep up appearances, and they would like to be part of their glittering processions.

You doubt this? Then look at what people who believe in religions statues have done to Jesus, and to themselves. It is true that they often show him in his starkest reality, dying, and with only a loin cloth and a crown of thorns. But they also show him with rich robes and expensive jewels. Their leaders have joined in his train, clothed with ermine and silk and velvet and wearing jeweled rings of gold. They too are crowned with high crowns glittering with the gems of every continent. "First class," they say. "The people expect it."

But Jesus says that their values are distorted. It is not that he is against silk and velvet or silver and jewels, or that he is against jet airplanes, white stallions, or classy automobiles. He would even bless these in their places. What he is against is pretense of any kind, and he is saying with his whole life, "Look, being a king does not depend on such things. True kingship comes from quite a different source. It comes from within, not from without; and it comes from reality, not from pretentions."

The true king is one who naturally identifies with the masses. I say "naturally" for it must be an unpretending honest identification. It is not merely a token identification, the parlaying of unctious talk into a false image, a kind of manufacturer of synthetic appeal. All of these seem to work for worldly kings, but none of them really works. In the end there is a great crashing fall for all pretenders. True kingliness depends on real identification between leaders and people. A great leader is of the people, by the people, and for the people. He is not royalty merely wearing the uniforms of the people, rather he is the people bearing the demeanor of royalty. Maximilian and Carlotta could not rule Mexico for the simple reason that they belonged to the Bourbons of Austria. They were very Bourbon and not even to the slightest degree even Mexican, much less very Mexican.

Jesus Christ is very God. John said of him, "In the beginning was the Word, and the Word was with God, and the Word was God" (John 1:1). Yet he sent for a donkey. It was not a gesture of pretense, a public relations maneuver to gain the attention of the people. Rather it was a natural expression of his reality as very man. Very

God, yes; very man, also yes.

This cosmic humility turns up in many different places in his life. He once told his disciples to go to the foot of the table at a banquet, and not to presume to sit at the head until asked. He taught the 5,000 and then fed them, breaking the fishes and the loaves with his own hands. He didn't own anything at all and once said, "The foxes have their holes and the birds have their nests, but the Son of man has nowhere to lay his head." He washed the feet of his disciples with his own towel. He was crowned King of kings with a crown of thorns. All of this is in keeping with the donkey.

Only one king in British history has borne the title. "Great." His name was Alfred, a man who wanted to be a servant more than he wanted to be a king, and who lived with the common people, and not the lords. In the end all the people, both small and great, followed him, and England was saved from the Danes. To this day the name "Alfred" means "true nobility." He got that way—not by pretending to be a servant, but by being a servant. He claimed Jesus Christ as his example and his inspiration.

Sending for the donkey was not a mere gesture. It was not an effort to hoodwink the people. No, there was nothing shyster about Jesus. He sent for the donkey because it was reality for him. He was not very God trying to be very man or very man pretending to be very God. He was truly both very God and very man. He sent for the donkey because his kingdom was different from all other kingdoms. It was not a kingdom of preference but of servanthood. He sent for the donkey because he was of the people, by the people, and for the people as much as he was of God, by God, and for God. He sent for the donkey because he was what he attempts to get all other men to be, manifestly himself.

"Bring me a donkey." Most of us find we cannot live like this, and the reason too often is that we are not real. We are a bundle of irrevocable pretensions built up from childhood, and we are those to whom appearances and seemings become securities. We hold all kinds of false ideas about how we should impress people—and everyone is surely trying to impress someone. Even the most extreme modern social cultists try to impress their peers, sometimes paradoxically, going "first class" by choosing "second class." For example, some of them wear faded and patched $25 blue jeans from the best store in town. How seeming can you get to be? Such people live not in the blazing clear light of the simple reality of God but in the light of their own selfish pretensions. If Jesus had not been of the people, by the people, and for the people, sending for the donkey would have been the boldest hypocrisy.

In Paul's language, the purpose is both to abase and abound, to know prosperity and poverty with equal grace, above everything else to be one's true self under God. What Jesus wants is no pretending. He wants bold reality. If it means to ride a donkey, ride a donkey. If it means to ride a golden chariot, then ride it; but above all, be authentic, be true, be real, be inwardly honest, and take your place as the servant of the people, for only the real authentic servants are truly "first class."

5

Appearances Are Secondary

> "Blind Pharisee! Clean what is inside the cup first, and then the outside will be clean too!" (Matt. 23:26, TEV).

In the passage from which these words are taken Jesus spoke both sharply and compassionately. He pierced the soul to lay bare the secret sin of the Pharisees, and then he turned from the formal plural to the compassionate singular "with increased earnestness and a certain friendliness of tone as one who would gladly induce the person addressed to mend his ways." [1]

Already within the shadow of the cross, he knew that his death was for all men, including the Pharisees, the very ones whom at the moment he confronted so fiercely. He knew, too, that the love of God for all men was the reason for his death. This near the cross, he would not stoop to rancor and bitterness. He cried out as loving father and compassionate physician, and he spoke as one warning against the clutches of heroin. He probed deeply, pointing out the causes and the cure of the terrible addiction. "Look, look," he seems to say, "your soul is sick with a terrible disease. You keep washing the outside, but the way to wholeness is to wash the inside. Cleanse first the inside, then the outside will be clean."

The true believer finds this truth easy to understand for he knows that the spirit of God does indeed cleanse from the inside. People of the world, however, not only reject it as truth for their own lives, they also deny it for others. Appearances are primary, many of them insist, and they believe that their salvation consists mainly of the right labels and the right uniforms!

They are like a wedding gift that Mabel and I received. It was a beautiful, perfumed, embroidered pillow, but when the perfume faded, it had a bitter, sour smell. Inside we found filth and vermin. The gift symbolized the giver herself, outwardly attractive and careful of the amenities but inside a bundle of contradictions. But like the Pharisee, she had built her life on pretenses and had never realized her true self. She covered her true self with all kinds of superficial and enslaving adornments. Kindly Jesus speaks to such people. "Cleanse the inside of the cup," he says. He wants them to see that seeming to be is sickness and being is wholeness.

Seeming to be is sickness. The Pharisees lived by outward appearances. Seeming to be was more important to them than being, and it led to dark subtle sins. Their values were misplaced, for they stressed the gifts on the altar more than they stressed the altar itself or the Temple. They had no creative evangelistic power, making of others proselytes instead of children of God. They flew false colors, openly honoring the prophets but inwardly secretly decrying them. They forgot the spirit of truth and rigorously kept minor laws while failing in justice, mercy, and faith. Jesus penetrated their hypocritical shells and called them whitewashed tombs, beautiful on the outside but full of dead men's bones.

Full of dead men's bones—this is a sharp poetic picture for seeming and pretending. It is an easy way to live, for outside structures are always less difficult to keep up than inside experiences. Highly visible exterior seeming requires less precision of honesty than interior being.

By merely seeming to be, man distorts the purity and simplicity of his central personality. He covers up the simple essence of his soul with evasion and self-deception, hiding as it were himself from his own eyes. In seeming to be when he is not, he is sick with himself, though he may not know it. It is easier for him to accept what others say he is than it is to be what God made him to be.

A very sad sight is to see a tiny Amish boy as the drab carbon copy of his father, as if the uniform was more important than the child. An even sadder sight is to see the Amish boy in rebellion against his father, accepting without understanding or discrimination the uniform of the outside world. In both cases, the boy is wrong. He merely changes from pretensions set by his family to pretensions set by others. In either case, he does not solve his problems of becoming and being, and among youth in general this is one of the major tragedies of our times. They rebel against one set of strictures imposed by the home only to become slaves to another set imposed by their peers. In the name of freedom, they become slaves. They are true Pharisees preoccupied with seeming and Jesus says to them, "Cleanse the inside of the cup."

The Jesus way is a better way: it is to come naked and unadorned before God and to find out what you were meant to be, not in the light of your wisdom but in the light of his grace. Real life begins with an intimate life-to-life touch of the soul with the spirit of God. It is fundamentally an awakening to responsibility under God, an awareness of self before God, and a surrender of self to the purposes of God. It is man in his simplest personal context: a face-to-face meeting with God in which he discovers and surrenders to the truth about himself. It sets aside demands of neighbors and teachers, of brothers and sisters, of friends and companions, and it focuses on one thing, the self under God.

In this simple transaction—the self under God—the personality emerges whole and directed. It never again has to answer to false standards and false demands. If Jesus said anything loudly and clearly, it was "Be yourself under God." "Take up your cross and follow me." When one does this, he opens himself to a being that is a becoming, to a life that grows and matures. Otherwise, he wanders about in continuing spiritual adolescence. In escaping the sickness of merely seeming, he can wear with grace either the black hat of the Amish or the blue jeans of his peers.

But woe to the sick man who goes on living out his Amish hat, or his blue jeans or his crew cut, or his long hair without ever truly finding his own personal wholeness in God. If he lives by labels and uniforms, he is a Pharisee—a whitewashed grave full of dead men's bones, and sick with his own being.

In seeming to be, a man is also sick with sin, and his sin is a great deal more than the sins most people see in the Ten Commandments. These, of course, are the fundamental sins, but so briefly stated, they are only points in an outline. Perhaps it is better that the outline is not fully filled out. Law tends to particularize sin so that man is tempted to see as not sinful the sins not specifically mentioned in the law.

Law is relative to the time and place of a specific evil deed, and often loses its significance for those general sins which frequently are much more violent and damaging than specific ones. Sometimes it seems that the more laws man makes, the more he stresses the letter of the law,

APPEARANCES ARE SECONDARY

and the less its spirit. The very language of law is literalism, and it works against the principle of obedience in spirit. To put it plainly, the more man solely lives by laws he makes the sicker he gets, mainly because his laws lose their divine and moral content. The same thing can be said of many religious customs and church practices.

The real point with many people is "Have I kept the law?" not as it should be, "Have I done right?" Like the Pharisees, such people are pretenders. They tithe the turnip seeds and forget justice, mercy, and faith. The sickest of all men are those who say only "Have I *seemed* to keep the law?" which means, "Have I kept up my pretenses?" In either case, their sickness is the lack of a meaningful inwardness, the lack of a true spiritual life.

Jesus wants us to see ourselves as we are on the inside, as slaves to emptiness and sterility, filled at times with self-disgust, boredom, and obsessions, and tempted to fear, filled with insincerity, aimlessness, and ultimately possessing the wish to die. These are the dead men's bones we try vainly to whitewash.

They are also the foul cement of the shells of hypocrisy we build about ourselves. They are responsible for the little Amish boy seeking refuge in the bright colors of the outside world; and for the minister's daughter openly defying her parents by living in open marriage, and flaunting her sin in their faces. She does not want to do it, but the demons of pride have overcome her, and because she is not clean inside, her very sin itself is a hypocrisy.

These inward sins are the sins of the broken man, the sins of the sick personality hiding from God. They are the pockmarks of the deadly syphilis of the soul, and they show both on the inside and the outside of life. These are the sins that spell mortal sickness for the whole of life. They control every word, shape every deed, mark every interpersonal transaction, and stain every thought. These inside stains are responsible for the outside scars. The filth and vermin of the feathers smell through the gayly decorated cover. Merely changing the cover or washing off the dirt is not enough to purify the whole. The sickness is inward and Jesus says, "cleanse the inside of the cup."

Being is wholeness. Jesus wanted the Pharisees to be truly themselves not what their tedious and contradictory laws made them. Not once did he renounce law or the idea of law, but he went to great pains to show that it had a divine and moral content, a spiritual meaning that was much more important than its mere letter. He saw the Pharisees as wooden robots controlled by their outward understanding of things. He wanted them to be answerable to an inner wholeness and not the robot strings of outwardness. As long as they minded the strings, they would not be authentic human beings. Only when they became men without strings could they stand up as true men. "Cleanse the cup," he said, "and the strings will vanish."

False being is not true being. The strings we let our false leaders tie to us keep us from true being. A girl rebelled against her middle-class parents for being "false and hypocritical." She could not stand their style of life, so she lost herself in the world of wandering youth. One day she wrote that she was coming home. Her folks met her at the bus and saw a girl: dirty, emaciated, drug addicted, and dying with a pitiful newly born baby in her arms. They received her with loving arms only to be told that they were false arms. They gave her and her child tender care only to be told that they did not mean it. They offered her clean new clothes only to be told that they were "bourgeois and poison."

APPEARANCES ARE SECONDARY

She disappeared again with her child into the dark black world of total nonconformity, wearing the conformity uniform of nonconformity, beads, jeans, sandals, and a blouse without a brassiere, smoking pot, and shooting heroin. All these were her robot strings pulled by a mad, empty people who try to escape one type of conformity merely to put on another type. Jesus would call them the blackest hypocrites of all—Pharisees, moral derelicts, clouds without rain, wells without water.

This seems to be the history of mankind, frantically going from one kind of false being to another, concerned wholly with seeming. Such people have yet to see that it is the inside of the cup that matters, and this not merely the self under self-scrutiny—this way is also totally false—rather the self under the eye of God. The miracle of true self-discovery begins when God steps into the picture, and until then, it is only a picture of frantic flight from one set of robot strings to another. Responsibility under God is the only way man can be free from the maze of robot strings that the world fastens upon him.

True being starts on the inside. "First cleanse the *inside* of the cup." The inwardness of man is important to God because that is where he wants to live. Indeed, as both Jesus and Paul taught, his true temple is the body of man. Perhaps one reason he wants the inside cleansed is that he prefers to live with health instead of sickness and with wholeness instead of brokenness, with truth instead of falseness. Jesus also knows that the contempt, the malice, the envy, the fear, and the greed inside a man are what destroys his relationship outside. He once said, "It is not what goes into a person's mouth that makes him unclean; rather, what comes out of it makes him unclean" (Matt. 15:11, TEV).

True being is the discovery of self under God. This at first seems to cut across the teaching that we are to forget self under God, but no place in the New Testament are we asked to forget self. The stress is on putting self in the proper perspective. "Seek ye first the kingdom of God, and his righteousness; and all these things shall be added unto *you*" (Matt. 6:33). Paul said, "*I* am crucified with Christ: nevertheless *I* live" (Gal. 2:20)—self under God, self completely surrendered to God, self following the direction of God. True being is to begin with the "naked I"—the self receiving itself as a gift from God, unadorned, and completely open. This is the meaning of repentance, the "I" turning from everything else to God.

As a child I had to wear the clothing of a dead cousin. This came near wrecking me psychically, because nothing fit, and in his clothing I was not me. Soon I got to thinking that because my cousin died, I, too, would die. In a sense I was living a lie, and it was making me spiritually ill. This is what happens to one who is not truly himself under God. One must live his own truth under God: not to live it is to be spiritually ill; to live it is to be spiritually whole.

A man can exploit his own uniqueness and his own talents—his own special truth from the outside of the cup and by saying, "This is how I want to develop," but this is finally to fail. He must do it from inside the cup by saying, "What does God expect me to do with what he has given me?"

True being is the acknowledgement of Jesus Christ as the power of God unto the salvation of self. He gave us the word, "First cleanse the inside of the cup." He is the power of that cleansing, and in fact, he himself is the cleansing. In one of his stories, he told of a man who swept his house but nothing entered it, and soon it was worse than it was at the beginning. For the house to be truly cleansed, it had to be filled; and for our cup to be cleansed, it too has to be filled.

Jesus offers himself as the Water of life to cleanse us and to fill us by refreshing and empowering us. He is whole, without disease, and without death. In him we have our deliverance; in his filling of our cup there is health and wholeness. The more we are open to him the more complete we become. He helps us to discover that we are ourselves, and not others, and that we have a name and that he gave it to us, and that we have a future and that he is it, and that in cleansing the inside of the cup, he also cleanses the outside.

6

When Confession Rings True

> "Not every person who calls me, 'Lord, Lord,' will enter into the Kingdom of heaven, but only those who do what my Father in heaven wants them to do" (Matt. 7:21, TEV).

A woman loses her grip on her skillet and it falls to the floor. She cries, "Lord, Lord"—that's profanity. A man is threatened with the loss of his job. Quietly at his desk, almost under his voice he says, "Lord, Lord"—that's a prayer. A church member, callous and ugly with hidden sin, sings with the congregation, "Lord, Lord"—that's hypocrisy. A gambler rolls his dice and says, "Lord, Lord"—that's perversion. A devoted youth bows his head in surrender to God's will and says, "Lord, Lord"—that's worship. So it becomes obvious that the words, "Lord, Lord" can be spoken with many different meanings and inflections.

Jesus knew this, and he warned that saying them can be a terrible pretension, even an evasion of the deeper requirements of the kingdom of God. One has only to study the uses of the word "Lord" in the Bible to see that this is true. Sometimes it means no more than "Sir," and conveys nothing of surrender or fidelity as when Thomas said, "My Lord and my God" (John 20:28, TEV). Sometimes it means only "Master" or "Commander" or "Owner."

Paul used it to represent the name of Jesus Christ. At

WHEN CONFESSION RINGS TRUE

the time of his conversion he cried, "Who art thou, Lord?" (Acts 9:5). Later he wrote that the world has many "lords," "Yet for us there is one God, the Father, from whom are all things and for whom we exist, and one Lord, Jesus Christ, through whom are all things and through whom we exist" (1 Cor. 8:6, RSV).

Early Christians used the phrase, "Jesus is Lord" in their worship. They picked it up from the New Testament writers who used it not merely as a title of authority and ownership, but in the sense of the Absolute and the Ultimate. Jesus was Sovereign, Preserver, and Protector. Paul called him, "Lord of lords" (1 Tim. 6:15) and "Lord of glory" (1 Cor. 2:8). John called him "the Lord God" (Rev. 1:8, RSV). Peter simply called him "Lord" (Matt: 16:22), but of course Peter's meaning was absolute for he also said, "You are the Christ, the Son of the living God" (Matt. 16:16, RSV).

Names have meanings, and usually when a man's name is spoken much more is implied than the few letters with which it is spelled. Speak the name "Lincoln," and one remembers the legends and events that have accumulated in his background, his prairie years and his war years, his wisdom and his suffering, his leadership and his death. Speak the name "Washington," and one gets a vast view of a very great leader. Speak the name "Benedict Arnold," and one has still another view of another kind of human being.

"Lord, Lord," as applied to Jesus Christ brings to mind a flood of memories not only of his words and deeds but of what men have said about him. Behind that name are such terms as "only begotten Son" (John 3:16), "Lamb of God" (John 1:29), "the Word" (John 1:1), "the effulgence of his glory" (Heb. 1:3, ASV), "the very image of his substance" (Heb. 1:3, ASV), "great high priest" (Heb.

4:14), "the author of their salvation" (Heb. 2:10, ASV), and many, many more.

So when we pronounce the name "Lord, Lord," we are making a confession. To say it is to declare our allegiance to the eternal God shown to us in the eternal Christ. It is to confess to the miracle of God's entrance into the life of man, the miracle of his creative omnipotence, the miracle of his reconciling love, the miracle of his redemptive wisdom. It becomes clear that the confession of the lordship of Christ is the first word the Christian must speak.

The word of surrender must be spoken. Confession is a promise of loyalty, yet it is much more. When made to Jesus Christ, it is the delivery of one's life to do his will. If it is spoken with reservation or doubt, it may not be the pure word of confession. If it is spoken incompletely but honestly, it is acceptable, for he recognizes the shortcomings of man. However it is spoken, the speaking one must realize that it is much like being born or adopted into a nation. Once the oath is given, his new allegiance becomes the dominating milieu of his life. The confession is not a mere word but an act, a conversion, a spiritual metamorphosis, wherein one achieves a new relationship.

In the confession, the confessor becomes an insider with God. No longer is he separated and estranged, no longer is he like a lost sheep outside the fold. Through confession he is the lost sheep brought home, and he is a newborn babe and a son, and miraculously he turns from death to life. Paul makes this plain, "If you confess with your lips that Jesus is Lord and believe in your heart that God raised him from the dead, you will be saved" (Rom. 10:9, RSV). John sustains him, "Every spirit which confesses that Jesus Christ has come in the flesh is of God" (1 John 4:2, RSV).

WHEN CONFESSION RINGS TRUE

Yet it must be kept in mind that every confession is not a true confession. It is possible for one to give an oath with reservation or doubt, or to give it and not mean it. It is also possible for one to deceive himself, that is to swear loyalty to God's kingdom without the slightest idea as to the nature and the requirements of that kingdom, and to go through life pretending to be a follower, yet not knowing that he is only a pretender. He can become so occupied with "seeming to be" that he misses the way to "becoming" and "being." He goes through all the formalities, but he does not touch the realities of God's kingdom.

Here we come very close to the meaning of this text, "Not every person who calls me, 'Lord, Lord,' will enter into the Kingdom of heaven." Jesus once told the story of a man with two sons. One said he would obey his father and didn't, the other said he wouldn't and did. Jesus made it very clear that the latter was the accepted one. There is something even in rebellion, a condition that leads to the kingdom. It is the condition of absolute sincerity, a sincerity that is proven by action. Saul of Tarsus, the persecutor of Christians, was wrong but sincerely searching. His earnestness led to truth. This is not to say that sincerity can bypass confession, but only that sincerity may lead to confession. It also suggests that the authenticity of confession is sincerity. If a man addresses Jesus Christ as "Lord," he must mean it, else he becomes the blackest of hypocrites.

It is also true that the confession "Lord, Lord," can become a false front for formality and tradition. This was what Jesus saw in the Pharisees. They erected a man-made religion and credited it to the Lord. Their creation was an unholy material thing which had lost its power to change life. These men cried, "Lord, Lord" to God, yet the religious framework they defended did not even remotely represent God. They did not realize the point which Herschel H. Hobbs makes, "The Kingdom is not words but deeds. It is even more than deeds. It is a spirit, a relationship to the King." [1]

A child may cry out, "Father," but the cry does not make him a son. Yet a true son also will cry out, "Father." True sonship comes only when the Father has confirmed the confession. He hears it from the heart, and he pronounces it authentic according to the deeds of the one crying out.

The word of surrender must be proven. Jesus put it sharply, "Only those who do what my Father in heaven wants them to do" (Matt. 7:21, TEV). One must get outside himself to find God's kingdom. This does not mean to forsake self, or to destroy self, or to impoverish self. Such approaches can be a terrible sickness of the soul. Rather it means to put self in the right perspective, to put self wholly under God, to turn from a service to self to service to others. It means a complete changing of mind, and of heart, and of will; it means to become a friend of God and of man.

One must do the will of God naturally. There can be no pretension or display in doing his will, advertising one's surrender as if to say, "Lord, look what a good boy I am." No, one does the will of God by being a good man wherever he lives, by whatever human context controls his life. He does the will of God by taking up his cross daily and bearing it with dignity and effectiveness. He does the will of God by becoming a man of meekness and of purity of heart.

He must not be too much concerned with a precise

knowledge of the will of God. It is very difficult to live up to all the options and to select one as the exact will of God. One may be able to say that he has found the will of God only after he has ventured an uncertain path. It is then that the word of faith is spoken, "This is the will of God; I am doing it." After all, as Dr. Hobbs says, the kingdom is deed, spirit, and relationship. One knows the will of God in living out the kingdom. *Living* the will of God is always moving forward in faith; *knowing* the will of God is usually looking backward to see how God has led one through trouble and temptations to the present hour. Because of what it has been in the past he knows what it will be in the future.

We know this—God's will always turns us toward our fellowmen, not away from them. In the New Testament, the early Christians were not wholly occupied with worship. As they were transformed under the lordship of Christ, they shared also their material possessions with others. And so it has been ever since, wherever there is a genuine Christian under the lordship of Christ, there is a person at work helping others.

John Wesley taught that beyond the necessities of life, one ought to use his money "in doing good to others." Dwight L. Moody, the evangelist, in his personal work in Chicago always asked, "Do you have food, clothing, and fuel?" It seems clear that the will of God not only makes one Christian responsible for his neighbor, it makes all Christians together responsible for all their neighbors.

Doing what God wants done is both easy and hard. It is hard because one must answer his conscience. Once Jesus said, "If any man's will is to do his will, he shall know whether the teaching is from God" (John 7:17, RSV). God's kingdom is indeed a kingdom of spirit, deeds, and relationship. When a man seeks God, asking in the Spirit, God will answer in the Spirit, and the man will see his way to go. Yet this is hard, very hard, for it requires him to be transfigured into God's realm in a way that detaches him from his earthly milieu. Yet in the detachment he finds reality, for always, invariably without exception, God's Spirit directs him back to service to his fellowmen.

Doing God's will is easy in that once it is found one has power from God to help him do it, yet it is hard because too often he looks for it in the light of his own wisdom and not in the light of the wisdom of all his brethren. It is folly for one man to assume that the whole world is his burden. God expects him to do his part, but most of all he expects him to work with his brethren as together they do their part.

The church must also confess, "Lord, Lord," and it must also do the will of God. The Great Commission was to the church, not just individuals. It was to the corporate body not merely to lone persons. The will of God is never completely done until all Christians do it together.

This is not to argue salvation by works or corporate salvation. James said, "Faith without works is dead" (Jas. 2:26). Faith must be proved with works. Paul said, "Bear ye one another's burdens" (Gal. 6:2). The authentic dimension of my personal confession is proved by how much of my neighbor's burden I carry and how deeply I enter into the wider community of well-doing.

These things are hard to believe, yet there they are peeping out at us from inside the text. Remember this, if doubters look in, doubters look out. If apostles look in, apostles look out.

7
Man's Ultimate Failure

"For many are invited, but few are chosen" (Matt. 22:14, TEV).

Jesus said, "*Whosoever* believeth in him should not perish" (John 3:16). He also said, "Come unto me, *all* ye that labour . . . and I will give you rest" (Matt. 11:28). *Whosoever* means every one and *all* means total. These are universal calls, yet Jesus also said, "For many are called, but few are chosen" (Matt. 22:14). Many sincere students of the Scriptures have been uncomfortable in the presence of these strange words. They have asked, "How can the love of God shut out any person, whatever the offense?" And to evade the hard truth, they have devised all kinds of interpretations for this text.

Some have said that all are saved, but to different levels of salvation—all are called, a few are chosen, but all are in the Kingdom. Others have seen in these words a hard double predestination. They have said that some are predestined to be saved, and some are predestined to be lost. And others have said that the words are spurious, that Jesus did not really say them. And still others that they applied only to the immediate situation and have no significance for the future followers of Christ.

On the other hand, other students have accepted the realism of the text. Matthew Henry said, "Many are called with a common call, that are not saved with a saving choice."[1] Frank Stagg said, "Many are invited, but not all approved."[2] The hard truth is that the text means what it says, "Many are called, but few are chosen."

Many shall be called. The universality of God's calling is clear. Isaiah said, "Ho, *every one* who thirsts, come to the waters" (Isa. 55:1, RSV). There is a spiritual emptiness in the heart of man that is akin to thirst. The more it goes unsatisfied, the more broken is man's personality. There is a sense in which we may say that the neurotic restless person is one with an unrequited need for God. The longer he remains unfulfilled, the farther from being a whole person he is, but his filling with the life of the Spirit turns him toward God in adoration.

The true becoming of man is his answer of God's call to him, and the mark of his becoming is his true worship of God—worship, with himself as the living sacrifice. Isaiah addressed this need for worship: "Come buy . . . without money." Jesus addressed it, "Whoever drinks of the water that I shall give him will never thirst" (John 4:14, RSV). He left no man out of his call. "Come," he said, "all ye that labour and are heavy laden, and I will give you rest." This sounds easy, but be warned, his calling is hard, very hard indeed.

It is a call to turn around. Man is fascinated with whatever looks away from God, and he spends most of his life with his back to God. God is light, but man loves darkness. God is perfection, but man loves imperfection. God is truth, but man loves error. God is righteousness, but man loves iniquity. God is the "wholly other" but man loves himself. God is wholly future, but man loves the past. God is life, but man loves death. Man misses the mark because he does not see the mark—his eyes are turned

MAN'S ULTIMATE FAILURE

in the wrong direction; so Jesus asks him to turn around. In a sense, this call to turn around is a call to see.

Man's horizon is too often only himself, and all he sees is death, but Christ says, "Look, look at me. I am Life, and if you look at Life you will see, and if you see, you will live." Some people reading these words will find them empty, while others will find them full; the truth is some see, some do not. Those who see find a well of life springing up within them. They will find more than the mere gifts of God—they will find God himself—a Presence that leads the seeing one to participate in that Presence, and to find it a shaping, loving, blessing Presence. The call of Christ is for all to turn around. Those who answer come into the light, those who do not answer, linger in darkness.

It is a call to come. God's movement toward man must be answered with man's movement toward God. God's movement is a speaking of man's name, a crying out to him. It is more than a word. It is the Word, the "Word made flesh." (See John 1:1-14.) The coming of the Word was a call to our coming. He said, "I am come that they might have life" (John 10:10). His death was also a call to our coming, "And I, when I am lifted up from the earth, will draw all men to myself" (John 12:32, RSV). Coming is really a part of the turning around, and it means to leave the dark and walk toward the light. One of the mysteries of turning is that when we turn we usually see only a little light, but the more we come, the more light we see.

Another mystery is that in coming we are becoming. Not only do we leave the dark, but we ourselves in coming are changed from darkness to light. The world sees only things, because it sees in the dark, but as we turn around to come toward God, we see in the light, and seeing in the light, we see that spirit is more than things. Going forward in faith, we come to the life of the spirit, and in this as did the prodigal son, we come to ourselves. In coming we find the real I in God, we discover God's ideal for us. We take up our cross, that is, we become real; we put aside all hypocrisy, all seeming, all fantasy, accept ourselves, and stand whole before God. This is not the purification of feeling but the purification of acceptance. It is not the living of someone else's experience, but the coming into our own experience. It is not the hypocrisy of constant self-purging, but the true becoming of faith.

It is a call to follow. God confronts the world in Christ, and points to him as the way of life, and says simply, "Follow him in the way." The call is to objective following. If his way is to feed the poor, then that is our way, if to visit the sick, that is our way too. The hard concrete reality of the call is that we must be the doers of the Word, but the trouble is that we would much rather be subjective in our religious experience. We would much rather talk about religious feeling than to engage in Christian action, and we would much rather tie our salvation to an experience of the past than to an active of the present.

This does not mean that the Christian experience is without the subjective, for surely turning around is subjective and coming is subjective, but following is objective. We must be careful, for following is not merely an action, it is an assumption, an appropriation, and a manifestation. Following is the everlasting completion of the becoming process, and it has its subjective side in that the Christ we follow is the Christ within us. Following Christ, the world sees less of us and more of him, for our real self nature is wholly his and wholly related to him.

MAN'S ULTIMATE FAILURE

We must conclude that the call of Christ to man is a radical call. The simple words—turn around, come, follow—are both easy and hard. They are easy for one whose pride is broken by the realization that he is standing in the presence of the real and sovereign God, and that *against him* he has no will and is not a man, but *in him* man's will is fortified by God's will, and he becomes man indeed.

The call is hard for the stubborn man whose pride of self is his most cherished possession, and who clings to his unbroken will as the evidence of his manhood. His personal tragedy is that if he does not willingly break his own will to God's favor, it will be broken sooner or later by a thousand lesser things, and yet he still cannot break it for God. The call to Christ is indeed a hard call.

Few are chosen. The setting of the text is a simple story. A king prepares a wedding feast and many people are invited, but only a few accept. Jesus says that the kingdom of God is like this, "Many are called, few are chosen." In the light of the story, the unchosen ones are those who deliberately did not accept the invitation. Some went to their farms, some to their businesses, and some made war on the king's servants. They willed not to come.

The meaning seems clear enough: men do not come to Christ because of a fearful obstinancy of will and stubbornness of soul. Christ chooses only those who choose him. Like a girl taking a husband, in the end she accepts the man who accepts her.

But why are men so obstinate and so stubborn? And why do they not accept God's invitation to the great banquet from which all the fearful ghosts of human existence are banished—death, suffering, and evil; and where eternal life and the eternal kingdom are offered only for the taking? Why do they reject the table of God set solely for them?

The answer is that man finds it almost impossible to surrender his own autonomy to the autonomy of God. He insists on being himself a god, and even in a fleeting moment when he considers coming to God, he had this funny idea that the way one enters God is to open the door and walk in. He does not understand that God has planned it another way, and that the way is for him to open wide all the doors of his life and let Another Man enter him.

The Another Man who comes in is a very special man, sometimes called "the Son of man," sometimes "the Son of God," and sometimes "Christ the Savior." But we who so bravely claim to be the master of our own destinies, the keepers of our own souls, the makers of our own lives—do not want Another Man inside of us to help take over these things; we would rather fail being our own master than to succeed with the help of Another Man inside of us.

Yet this is precisely what happens, failure or success, death or life, according to who is the ruler of our lives— ourselves or the Son of man. The apostle Paul put it plainly, "Do you not understand that Christ Jesus is within you? Otherwise you must be failures" (2 Cor. 13:5, Moffatt).[3]

One of the notions of today's world is that "I must be my own man." And if I surrender to anything except the "I" within me, I am not myself. This is a half-truth. The "I" within me is an imperfect I, and if alone it is followed, it leads to death. Christ is the perfect other man who becomes my captain. In him I become my own true man, and in him I find perfected autonomy. In him I lose all and gain everything.

MAN'S ULTIMATE FAILURE

Man's stubbornness against sharing his life with Christ in him keeps him from the banquet. He cannot enter in to God because he will not let Jesus Christ enter him. He nails the doors of his life against any intrusion, and defies anybody to open them. This is his choice, and this is his undoing.

8
Treasures of the Heart

"For your heart will always be where your riches are" (Matt. 6:21, TEV).

The Chinese have a proverb, "Man endlessly becomes himself." People from Missouri are sometimes heard to say, "The older we get the more like ourselves we become." These point to a truth that man has a difficult time accepting. It is that what a man is he chooses, and what he chooses, he becomes.

Some people insist that they can be right and choose wrong, or that they can be wrong and choose right. Of course, there are many examples where good people have made wrong choices and bad people good choices, but as a rule ultimately in the sum of life, wrong will choose wrong and right will choose right. If one is good, he becomes better; if he is bad, he becomes worse. This is one of the irrevocable rules of spiritual truth. Jesus put it plainly, "For your heart will always be where your riches are."

He spoke these words twice in his ministry. The first time in the heart of the Sermon on the Mount. Warning against thieves that steal and rust that destroys earthly treasures, he asked his listeners to "Lay up treasures in heaven." Three verses later he went to the heart of the matter, "You cannot serve God and mammon" (Matt. 6:24,

RSV). The great choice he put before man is between things and God. He believed that if a man reaches for things he will become like a thing, and if he reaches for God he becomes like God. Our personal choices are the sure compasses that lead us to our triumphs and our tragedies.

The second time he spoke these words was in another sermon in which he told the story of the rich fool who destroyed his barns to make bigger ones. Sated with his abundant crops he said to himself, "Soul, you have ample goods laid up for many years; take your ease, eat, drink, be merry" (Luke 12:19, RSV). God put in his appearance and said, "Fool, this night your soul is required of you." Then again Jesus told the people that where their treasures are, their hearts will be.

Rich toward self or rich toward God, which will it be for you? Reaching for self you become more and more like the wrong you have chosen for yourself; reaching for God you become more and more like his love. Man has a way of getting what he reaches for, not always exactly like he had dreamed it, but enough like it for us to conclude that what a man wants, man usually gets.

What a man wants, he usually gets. One is tempted to say what a man wants, he always gets, but there are too many cases of frustration and defeat which argue to the contrary. Many people wanted fortune who didn't get it, and many more wanted power who also failed. Yet, did they fail?

The proud heart is not necessarily only for those who gain wealth. It is possible for a pauper to be a miser, and for a peon to be a dictator. On the other hand, many wealthy people have not been misers, and many kings have not been dictators. The point here is to rightly answer the question: What is the ruling principle of your life? Is it wealth for wealth's sake or power for power's sake? Or is it the love for God and the love for man?

When I was a child, my family lived in the same block with a couple reported to be the poorest people in town. Yet their house and yard were filled with junk, things that other people discarded—bottles, papers, broken radios, cast-off clothing, tin cans, pieces of machinery, rusty nails, soiled mattresses, junk cars, odds and ends of lumber, and numerous other things. They guarded all this junk just like some people guard their bank accounts. What they lacked in true wealth they accumulated in false wealth. Since all wealth is relative anyway, it could be said of them that they truly got what they wanted. Their greed and their avarice became the controlling principles of their lives. It influenced their whole way of living and thinking. Some of their neighbors said they even looked like their junk.

In that same block lived another family who wanted only to be at peace with God and man, and to rear a responsible family. There were times when it appeared they would not make it. They lost their home, they were beset by illnesses, one child for a time was completely wayward, but in the end they were looked upon as the most respected family in their community. The way was long and hard, but they, too, got what they wanted.

Some people choose nothing, and they get it. Never quite able to make up their minds about their goals in life, they drift like children, unaware of reality, and snatching at fleeting daydreams. They ask little, they get nothing. Others asked for more out of life, and got more, not always exactly what they had dreamed but enough to satisfy.

What happens in the end depends on the things they

treasure most. Their dreams will lead them to find their true selves, often good, and just as often bad.

What a man gets, he becomes. Most people do not believe this. They think that all that talk from Jesus about not being able to serve both God and mammon is not true. They say, "Man can indeed have his cake and eat it too. He can profess to be seeking the kingdom of God, while pursuing the selfish desires of his own heart." When will they learn?

The long history of mankind puts the lie to their claim. Man becomes what he sows, and what he sows is himself. He reaps the vile fruit of his own bad character, and the power behind it is this irritating law of nature, "Where man's treasure is, his heart will be." Man shares the fate of whatever he gives himself to; if to the perishable, then the fate of things that perish; if to the imperishable, then to the things that perish not. In tiny invisible steps, one shadow upon another, the human heart takes into itself the styles and the natures of the treasures it seeks.

If one seeks only gold, his heart becomes cold metal; if only flesh, he dies as the flesh dies; if power, he perishes when others steal his power; if he seeks only fame, he will perish as others become more famous; if he seeks only ease, he will dry up and fade away. If he seeks fulfillment of his false selves, he will become a miserable creature always trying to conform to the false standards of this world.

Why does the needle in the compass turn north? Because the essence of the needle is the essence of the great northern lode. Why does the sunflower follow the sun? Again because the essences are the same. The proverbialist said it long ago, "The name of the Lord is a strong tower; the righteous man runs into it and is safe" (Prov. 18:10,

RSV). Yet in contrast, "A rich man's wealth is his strong city, and like a high wall protecting him. Before destruction a man's heart is haughty" (vv. 11-12, RSV).

Yes, what a man gets, he becomes. Let us drive the nail deeper by saying what a man becomes, he is.

What a man becomes, he is. Becoming can be a lifelong process. Little by little he hardens himself into whatever he finally is. He may not become what he would have been, and what he does become may not be the ideal self God gave him, but surely what he becomes, he is. Most of the time our true selves are covered by layers and layers of habits, eccentricities, defensives, attitudes, pretensions, hypocrisies, all carefully selected in keeping with our dreams and our ambitions. If the beginning was false, and if we selected our layers in keeping with ideas and ideals foreign to our true nature, then what we finally are is a monstrous bundle of imperfections. We slowly conform to an image that we hold. If it is a false image, the image of this world then underneath all our layers is a disease of the worst kind, the disease of fundamental self-deception which may be one of the worst sins of all.

Following World War II hordes of refugees came from the Iron Curtain countries into Germany. Some were prohibited from bringing out anything except the clothing they wore. The refugee authorities insisted on stripping and bathing immediately on entry. Layer after layer of clothing would come off, and with it the grime and filth of weeks of travel. Most wore rags and in the rags were lice and other vermin. Finally, they stood naked under the showers for cleansing and delousing. All were given clean new clothes. Some would turn away from their rags, never wanting to see them again. Others would bundle them and carry them about with them, and some would even wear them again in preference to their new garments. It could be said of them that some became new creatures and moved on to higher dreams, while others persisted in being their old selves and continued their ragged self-adornment. Some were becoming their truer and more fundamental selves, the others hiding their true selves in their diseased and dirty layers of false being. Some had lived in rags only until they could do better. Others had lived in rags until they became rags.

Whatever a man is, he becomes more like himself the older he gets. He goes on endlessly becoming himself. Sometimes this self is a false self, one different from what God dreamed for him. If he becomes bitter and selfish, hard to get along with and crude in his relationships, he may be reaping the by-products of all the things he treasured.

Treasure has become *the* treasure.

Jesus offers us a way out. He said, "Seek ye first the kingdom of God, and his righteousness; and all these things shall be added unto you" (Matt. 6:33). Paul reaffirmed this when he said, "All things are yours, whether . . . the world or life or death or the present or the future, all are yours; and you are Christ's; and Christ is God's" (1 Cor. 3:21-23, RSV). The truth of the matter is, things own us, unless we are owned of God. If we submit to the ownership of Christ, and if we let nothing else own us, then we can own all things in the only way we can truly own them, as responsible keepers of what belongs to others.

Your truest and highest being comes only as you strip yourselves of all pretensions and eccentricities and stand bare in God's presence, saying to him: "Thy will be done with me." Such a surrender to true being requires you "to present your bodies as a living sacrifice, holy and acceptable to God, which is your spiritual worship. Do not be conformed to this world but be transformed by the renewal of your mind" (Rom. 12:1-2, RSV).

The treasure of the kingdom of God, the gift God wants you most to have, the only way for you to live a whole and free life, is the treasure of your own true being. Smother it with false dreams, cover it up with high-minded pretensions, drown it with desires of the flesh, grind it to pieces with the lust for the world, pummel it and preen it, abase it and abound it, feed it on the empty husks of your exaggerated ego—all this and at the end torment. You finally and irrevocably become what you are. Your choices have condensed you. You possess all and have nothing.

On the other hand, strip your soul, cleanse it by repentance, bring it to God as an offering, seek its constant renewal from his Spirit—all this—and at the end, victory. You possess nothing and own all. God is the giver, you are the keeper.

Doesn't it make sense that it is better for man to always be growing toward his true self than his false self? If this is your conviction, then you know what it is to lay up treasures in heaven.

9

Let the Dead Alone

"Let the dead bury their own dead" (Luke 9:60, TEV).

"Unforgettable, mystic, hard," some have said of these words. Others have called them harsh and senseless. Yet we cannot forget them, and they pull at us for we suspect that though they speak of death, they mean life.

They are indeed hard to understand and lead people to create meanings not really found in the text. "Let the dead in spirit bury the dead in body" is one such meaning. This is an evasion and is not unlike the evasion of the scribe who first heard these words.

Another man offered to follow the Lord only to be told that the way would be hard and would lead to no place he could call home. Jesus then turned to the scribe and said, "Follow me." Appearing not to understand what the call meant, the man took a timid step forward and said, "But let me go first and bury my father." Then Jesus forbade him. His timidity turned into swift retreat. While he pondered, the crowd passed him by. He disappeared from our view, trapped between death at home and life from Jesus.

The scribe was face to face with one of the hardest truths of the New Testament. Chrysostom, the early Christian teacher summarized it: "Jesus forbade him to go in order to show that nothing, not even the important work of natural duty and affection, is so momentous as care for the kingdom of heaven."[1] Important as it is to bury the dead, there are more important duties, and God's work always comes first. Human responsibilities are less binding than divine ones. Christ comes first, even before family.

How can Jesus be so demanding?

How can one who teaches the law of love be indifferent to human need? Even the Jewish priests were not that callous, for they who ordinarily must avoid contact with the dead could always go home to bury their fathers. And Elijah before receiving Elisha as a follower permitted him to say goodbye to his father.

Was Jesus trampling human love? Had he pushed aside all pity? And how can these stern words be reconciled with his call to visit the prisoners in jail and to feed the poor? How can they be reconciled with his saying, "Greater love has no man than this, that a man lay down his life for his friends" (John 15:13, RSV) and with his demand that we love our neighbors as ourselves?

One thing is certain, the words are true. Jesus spoke them, and they have meaning for life. In speaking them, he confronted the scribe standing between his past and his future and torn between his duty and his vision. He gave him the opportunity of taking a step that could change him from being a life loser to becoming a life winner.

Jesus pressed the scribe to do the thing he least wanted to do: to make a firm decision that would forever break him loose from the past and hurl him into the future. "Follow me," he said. "Leave the dead to bury their own dead"—you must choose, you must choose between death and life, and if you choose life you must live. These are the moral challenges he gives to all of us and to the degree that we act positively in meeting them, to that degree we

LET THE DEAD ALONE

live—in both present experience and eternal reality.

You must choose. Personhood is important to Jesus. He approaches each man differently, and he approaches him decisively. Knowing the unfathomable depth of the mystery of the human soul, he calls them to awaken to themselves as believing living persons and to make clear-cut decisions that will lead them to find their real selves.

The stringency of his call can be seen in the sharpness of his words to his followers: to Nicodemus he said that he must be "born anew"; to Peter and Andrew, "Follow me, and I will make you fishers of men"; to the man paralyzed for thirty-eight years, "Rise, take up your pallet and walk." Without doubt, he confronts men with a challenge to choose decisively and irrevocably.

Men who cannot decide for themselves are men who cannot become. Their becoming, their flowering from the helplessness of childhood into the fruit of maturity and responsibility, is dependent on a firm decision to stand and to reach for the future. They must choose and not go on postponing year after year the manner of men they are to be. For example, if a young man painfully puts off his vocational decision, and is pushed about by the loose talk and suggestions of his friends—never standing on his feet, never deciding in the light of his real self, always imitating the styles of others, always dependent, always weak, never becoming, then to a measure that young man is always dying.

Jesus saw the scribe as such a man and doubtlessly realized that his refuge in death was itself an evasion. He probably also knew that even if the young man went home, his character was such that others would have to bury his father. There was not enough life force in him to carry his own weight. Jesus wanted the scribe to face himself and to become, and he knew it would take a hard decision for him to turn around. Jesus saw him as helpless and unfulfilled, and he pressed upon him decisiveness as a way of life. He said almost in the same breath, "No one who puts his hand to the plow and looks back is fit for the kingdom of God" (Luke 9:62, RSV). Jesus bestows manhood upon the deciders, not upon the equivocators.

Many people have difficulty in coping with responsibility. One of the characters in the play *Harvey* dreams of a vacation in which he can sit under a tree with plenty to eat and drink and with a beautiful girl to lay her soothing hand on his brow and say again and again, "Poor boy, poor boy." This sad creature was the abiding adolescent seeking refuge in the helplessness of childhood, living in his past at some point in his life where he did not have to be a responsible person, not growing, not contracting, not loving, not becoming, not even being—dead; yes, dead in spirit and dead in heart.

It is not uncommon for a man to plead a lesser duty in order to escape a greater one. The scribe was not indecisive because he was weak, but weak because he was indecisive. Jesus is teaching that real personhood grows out of a series of firm forward-looking decisions that lead us to our real duties and our real selves.

Choose between death and life. Whatever Jesus meant in these words, he did not mean neglect of parents, and he had not forgotten how to love. He probably knew what the behavioral scientists are just now finding out, that most people prefer to live in shells, hoping to escape the realities of themselves. Timidly they set a foot forth in the world, and then they retreat, refusing to make the firm decision that leads them to life. They prefer to live indirectly and indecisively and to retreat to death. They live in constant evasion of reality.

The words, "Lord, let me first go and bury my father," did not tell all the truth about this man's real character. Jesus saw him for a brief moment looking forward, and then hesitating, only to turn and face backward, refusing to face up to the duty and the facts of himself. "I want to go home," he might have said, "to the shell of my father."

We must be careful here and not assume that the father had made the shell. This can be true, but usually the toughest shell is the one the son makes for himself in an effort to escape his real self. Such shells are not imposed, but created by evasions. Much of the time they are assumed from a group in which the individual is trying to hide.

Seeing himself and not liking what he sees, he projects his weakness onto his father, and says, "I want to be free." He then joins a group and puts on its uniform. The new uniform or shell may be symbolized by freakish hair and dirty clothing, but the freedom he thought he wanted is only further smothered by the cliches and the outer garments of the new group. He becomes a robot of the group, taking up habits that are not in keeping with his true self.

Wearing a beret and a smock does not make one a painter. In fact, the best artists have not always worn berets and smocks. Yet there are always those unhappy people in schizophrenic conflict with the real self that God gave them who put on berets and smocks hoping to be painters. They are only evading themselves, and no man can prove himself by evading himself.

To evade one's true self, or to impose an artificial self upon one's true self is to retreat into the precincts of the dying. To try to set a direction for oneself without first accepting one's true self—or as we sometimes say, without making peace with oneself—is to make a false start. An even worse evasion is to face oneself and take a hesitant step forward, as the scribe did, and then fall back into oblivion. Either way, it is the dead burying the dead.

A choice for life is a choice for God. It is to accept the reality of the true self and to put it back in the hands of God for his development. This is a hard decision to make, because we have the illusion that in giving up our shells we give up ourselves. This is not true, for it is the shell that smothers and destroys, and it is the shell that keeps us from maturity and responsibility.

When we fight desperately and say, "I want to be free; I want to be me," we often mean the exactly opposite: "I don't want to be me. I want a nice artificial shell that is like someone else. I want a pretty whitewashing that keeps the real me from showing." This is like saying, "I would rather die than to live." For when we evade our true self—the self of a future in God—and follow the self that turns back into its shell, we are choosing death.

The possibility of evasion is always present, and it can work the other way around. "All the rest of the world wears rings in their noses, but in defiance I prove my freedom by not wearing a ring." Don't be fooled, the point of no ring may be a rebellion against what God meant you to be. If you wear a ring in your nose, or don't wear a ring in your nose, merely to prove your freedom and your difference, you are not really free; but if deep down you make peace with yourself and with God, the ring or the lack of rings is not what people see but that you are living and not dying.

Turning your back on your own real becoming, this is death, the dead burying the dead. Facing forward, coming naked to truth, offering yourself as a farmer offers an unknown seed to God, trusting the true life that he lodged in that seed, shedding all of your self-imposed shells, trusting his fire and his water, this is eternal life, the living raised from the dead. Jesus is the real choice, for he said, "I am the way, the truth, and the life."

No man can live the divided life as Kirkegaard so convincingly argued. Purity of heart, he said, is to will one thing. Above everything else it is to be true to yourself in Christ. "Come to me," Jesus said. "Come to life. Don't look back to Nineveh, don't go back to Egypt, come to life. Decide, make peace with the self God gave you, let it grow, let it contract, let it become. Decide, make your decision irrevocable, and claim life instead of death."

If you choose life, then you must live. There comes to most people a moment of inner understanding when they catch a glimpse of their own true essence, not wholly and not in clear detail, but dimly and fleetingly, a moment when they begin to understand the true meaning of their "I." It is as if in a flash the seed sees inside itself and says, "I know what I am, and I see as in a shadow what I was meant to be." Such an experience opens our way to the possibility of wholeness. Resolutely opening ourselves to Christ can make it happen, and the way we do this is through repentance and faith.

Repentance is often misunderstood. Many people have an idea that it means "to renounce sin." It does mean this, but it means so much more that to say it means only this is to almost totally miss its meaning. The word is from the Greek, *metaneo,* literally "turn around." When Jesus said, "Except ye repent ye shall all likewise die," he meant "turn around or die." This was the alternative he offered the scribe, "Turn around or die."

Jesus saw the young man chasing death for his shell.

His fleeting false turn never really meant anything, and it was like so many of our superficial conversions. The scribe saw the glory of Jesus and wanted to march in his army, but not to camp with him in the wilderness. He wanted the blessings without the disciplines, and he wanted to belong without changing. He wanted Christ to take him, shells and all, but Christ wanted him to come as he was, not with his shells.

When forced to choose, the scribe took up death. The close confining shell of always dying at first seems much more tolerable than the freedom in Christ of always living. Not to become is seemingly easier than to become. Burying oneself in evasions is easier than facing one's true self in God. In evading, one is always becoming death; in accepting, one is always becoming life.

The important thing is to realize that in coming open to Christ, eternal life is your gift now—not tomorrow, not at the end of your time on earth—but now, and one of the best proofs that you truly have eternal life now is that you live in community with all human beings. You don't go back to death, you go on to life—now.

As I write, I am aware of a tiny invisible vortex between the point of my pencil and the paper. In that vortex is *now*. What is written in the now lingers in the past, falling behind the moving pencil lead. What is in the now is the remembered past and the unborn future, except that Christ always stands before us in the future. Out of that future he offers us a special kind of life. He gives it to us from the other side of death, as one who could say, "I died, and behold I am alive forever more" (Rev. 1:18, RSV). To accept that life, we must turn our faces from death. We must stand up to live, gloriously aware of the blowing winds and greening grass, flying birds and blooming flowers, sensing, dreaming, growing, but above all, we must be sensitive to the face of God in our fellowman. We must live, hilarious in our thanksgiving that now we do indeed have life.

Christ standing before the scribe, stood in the future, calling the man forward to life, calling him to the true self God made him to be, to stand up and face God in a decisive manner, to stand to the full height of his manhood, to live. In short, he was asking him to believe—to believe that God confronts him in Christ with the challenge to live. Turning is an act, believing is surrender.

The scribe does not stand alone, for we stand with him. Christ speaks to us both from the past and from the future and in his Spirit. He is always calling to life, and even as I write these words, I sense his presence in time between when the word is not and is, and between the ticking and no-ticking of the clock on the wall. In the same way he comes to you in the now, between where your eye finds these words and where it finds them not, yes in the now, more than in time, in realization more than in experience. He stands as the life-bearer, and he wants you to live.

Blessed is he whose eyes are alive to see and whose ears are alive to hear, and sadly, let the dead bury the dead.

10
Harlots First

"The tax collectors and the prostitutes are going into the Kingdom of God ahead of you" (Matt. 21:31, TEV).

This sharp discriminating saying of Jesus has upset many "good" people, beginning with the Pharisees who thought of themselves as "better." Their life objectives seemed to be to take a place above other people—and to boast of it. In their view the worst man was a tax collector and the worst woman a harlot. When Jesus said, "Tax collectors and harlots before you," they were shocked into rage. It was too much for their pride, and they shouted out against him. The Pharisees were more concerned about preserving their proud community than they were about healing the wrong in the world. Their emphases were activity, labels, and position; they forgot the fundamentals of purpose, content, and direction. It was the old story, ever new, of pride going before a fall. Jesus stabbed them awake with simple words that signboard the mysterious power of his kingdom, "Harlots first!"

Stressing activity and forgetting purpose. Just before he spoke these hard words, Jesus told of a man who had two sons. He asked them both to work in the vineyard. One said, "I will not" and did; the other, "I will" and didn't. Jesus asked the Pharisees, "Which one did the will of his father?" They gave the obvious answer, "The first one."

We must ask of this parable, "Who are the *I wills* and the *I will nots?*" Jesus suggested the answers: The *I wills* are Pharisees of this world, and the people who stress the outward appearance, those who place more emphasis on seeming to be than on being, and who emphasize means more than ends. Their preoccupation is endless ceremonial activity without remembering that the real purpose of life is moral and spiritual improvement. They are always saying, "I will, I will," yet never really stand up for righteousness. The *I will nots* are the timid and the uncertain who are concerned with personal honesty, those to whom being true is more important than appearing true. Their preoccupation is with reality. They sometimes say, "I will not, I will not," yet they stand for what is right.

Modern man is probably as pharisaic as his forefathers. In business, his temptation is a beautiful office, a well-oiled organization, and a smooth job description, all of which may be good; yet preoccupation with them may lead to bankruptcy, because these are not the purposes of business. In education, the stress may be on methodologies which become so complicated and heavy that the student is forgotten.

A business can fail in the midst of its finest organizational hour. A school system can have the most modern buildings and the best techniques but produce high-school graduates who cannot read or write.

In a church, the "program," important as it is, can become its undoing. Little rules and regulations which become busy work may seem to work for a while and eventually come to be accepted as inexorable laws, yet all the while we may be forgetting people as people: a name becomes *a prospect,* a life change becomes *an addition,* and a human being becomes *a member.*

Pride in mere activity can lead only to the dulling of the sense of purpose.

Stressing labels and forgetting content. In an address to his disciples, Jesus said of the Pharisees, "They do all their deeds to be seen by men; for they make their phylacteries broad and their fringes long" (Matt. 23:5, RSV). Phylacteries and fringes are labels, and so accustomed is the world to their power that to see them is to become overawed by them. The gavels and robes of the judges, the maces or medallions of the college presidents, the honors and awards of the sportsman often overwhelm us.

Jesus wants men to see that it is not the label but the content that matters. It is a lesson deeply rooted in the Old Testament, for the second of the Ten Commandments says, "You shall not make for yourself a graven image" (Ex. 20:4, RSV)—nothing, no label, no image, no likeness, nothing shall stand between you and reality. Not your education, not your honors, not your badges and your uniforms, not your position, not the size of your office or your car, not the number of rooms in your house, not the rings on your fingers or the sizes of their stones, not your degrees, not your commissions and your trophies, not your ordination papers or your baptismal certificates, none of these phylacteries and these fringes mark your true manhood and your true womanhood. All of them may be comfortable for you, and they all can be worn with grace, but none of them really matter. What does matter is your moral and spiritual content: what you are inside, your purity of heart and mind, the quality of your life, and the depth of your commitment to reality and responsibility.

Stressing position and forgetting direction. When Paul advised the Roman Christians to "Be kindly affectioned one to another with brotherly love; in honour preferring one another" (Rom. 12:10), he was reflecting on one of the cardinal concepts of the Gospels. One cannot truly be good unless one is willing to honor other people. Preferring the first place, seeking the highest honors, acquiring the great trophies may be good American ambition, but it is not necessarily good Christian faith.

"The image is the thing" is a motto of depravity, and when applied to the human person, it reveals a pagan perversion of values. First places, highest honors, and trophies for their own sake can be sugar in your gasoline tank. They can gum up and destroy your true motivation. This is not to say you should not have them or that they are not important. That would be foolish. It is to say that having them as proof of what you are is terribly wrong. The prettiest girls do not always win beauty prizes, the smartest people do not always win the best scholarships, the best-qualified men do not always get the finest jobs. Surely, "the image is not the thing" when it comes to judging real character.

Jesus, by saying "Harlots are first" was trying to shock the Pharisees into seeing that their exalted positions did not necessarily mean that they were headed in the right direction, and that having the best seats in the synagogue and sitting at the head table at banquets do not mark the man as honorable and pure. This is hard medicine to take, but it does cure the soul.

At another time, to enforce this point, Jesus told of two men praying in the Temple, a Pharisee and a publican. One prayed loudly and proudly and in full view of men. The other prayed softly and lonely and in full view of God. Jesus then said, "I tell you, this man [the publican] went down to his house justified rather than the other:

for everyone who exalts himself will be humbled, but he who humbles himself will be exalted" (Luke 18:14, RSV). The important thing was not their station or position, but their direction. C. S. Lewis said that the kingdom of God is like a man on a bus dressed in rags but headed toward heaven, while another man finely dressed is on the wrong bus headed toward hell.

The point is not that the harlot was good and the Pharisee bad, but the harlot had truly repented and the Pharisee had not. The true Christian is one that can see evil in his own life and turn away from it. He must recognize that as Frank Stagg so succinctly says, "Radical demand and limitless mercy are brought together in the teaching and manner of Jesus." [1] When we realize the true meaning of "Harlots first," we will begin to translate that "radical demand" and that "limitless mercy" into our own daily "teaching" and "manner."

11

The Holy Option

"They are wrong about sin, because they do not believe in me" (John 16:9, TEV).

A man discovers a growth on his arm and calls it a wart. It changes color and bleeds. He says, "My wart is causing me a little trouble, but it will pass," and he forgets it. Later he finds that it is much larger and very black. His wife is alarmed and persuades him to go to his physician. The doctor speaks the dreaded words, "Cancer—melanoma." The man's attitude changes. Yesterday he saw the wart as a harmless growth and never gave it a second thought. Today he sees it as bigger than his life and thinks about it all the time.

The difference is conviction. The doctor came into his life and changed his mind by telling him the truth about himself. "You are wrong about that little growth. It is not a harmless wart as you think, but death. The only hope for you is to cut it out and to get rid of its poison." The doctor convicted the man of the terror of the wart because he had not yet done what was necessary to get rid of it. He was wrong about his wart because he had not seen the terrible cost of keeping it, or of getting rid of it. The doctor set it forth in a clear light—he made the man sensitively aware of his predicament, and he showed him a way to correct it. Something like this is the teaching of the text.

You are sick with sin and don't know it. You have missed the whole point on sin. You have missed it because you have followed blind guides such as false definitions, conscience, and law. None of these tell the whole truth about sin.

False definitions cause men to confuse sin with guilt. They lead them to follow some of the modern psychologists who concentrate on getting rid of guilt as if guilt itself was the sin. They say, "It is perfectly all right to live in adultery if one does not feel guilty about it." This is like saying, "If I will refuse to believe the wart is a cancer, it will be okay."

Murderers, thieves, rapists, arsonists are all guilty but they don't always feel guilty. It is not uncommon for a newspaper to report that a prisoner on trial was calm and collected and showed no sense of guilt, yet the crime was there, deep dark wrong against God and man. No amount of expunging of the feeling of guilt will expunge the effect of the crime. Calling a cancer a beauty spot does not destroy the death that is in it.

Sin is sometimes described as inconsequential, as an inevitable peculiarity of the human race, and necessary for man's well being. The *Playboy* philosophy contends that the real pleasures of life are the sensate ones: eating, drinking, and merriment. It holds that moral discipline is old-fashioned and perversion is normal. This has the effect of calling white black, sweet bitter, true untrue. The Holy Spirit warns us against this self-deception, showing us that sin is indeed sin and that it is responsible for all our misery. Yes, sin is the other side of all despair, all loneliness, all uselessness, all frustration, and all failure, and merely getting rid of our guilt about sin does not destroy its real influence. Calling a cancer a wart does not eliminate its poison.

Conscience plays tricks on a man's understanding of sin. The trouble is that man abuses his conscience. He defies it, bribes it, ignores it, suppresses it, deceives it, and crushes it until it becomes stupified and insensitive. Or if not this, he traps it with the faulty guidelines of his own proud autonomy. What he thinks is light is only his own inner darkness. The Spirit cries out to his conscience, "All have sinned and come short of the glory of God" (Rom. 3:23). This is sin—to fall short of the glory of God. One who measures himself only by his conscience is apt to see only a prejudiced compromise. The Spirit is the burning external light that puts the spotlight on reality.

Law speaks only of the outward acts of sin. Fully as important as conscience and having the clear function of isolating and categorizing sin, law still does not always speak to the sin of the heart. You can try a man for murder but not for pride; you can try him for stealing but not for prejudice; and you can try him for child abuse but not for blindness to truth. The plain fact is that law cannot touch the deeper recesses of sin. It cannot adequately deal with hate, jealousy, procrastination, indolence, indifference, greed, selfishness, secret imaginations, and the like; yet all these are sins sometimes fully as terrorizing as murder, theft, and rape. The Spirit deals with the deeper hidden sins, and when he falls upon a man, he truly convicts him of their terror. The man with the wart knew that cancers could mean death, that is, he knew the law on cancers, but he put it out of mind until the doctor pronounced him cancerous. The Holy Spirit prompts us, telling us we are sinners.

False definitions, conscience, and the law lead men to

think their personal warts of sin are different, that they themselves are exceptions, and that judgment cannot come to them. God recognizes the grasp that such blindness has on people. So he says something like this: "I send my Spirit to awaken you, to cause you to see yourself, to make you understand the penalty of sin, and warn you of its darkness. Above all, I send my Spirit to get you to turn around."

Your sin sickness means death. God speaks clearly to men: "You are wrong about sin. You think it is joy. I say it is sorrow. You think it is freedom; I say it is slavery. You think it is life; I say it is death." The Scriptures are plain on this point. "The wages of sin is death" (Rom. 6:23). We see examples of this in nature; if a man neglects a cancer, his body rots away; if he spends a lifetime drinking alcohol, his liver hardens and he dies; if he is a glutton, he develops heart trouble and diabetes; if he plays with a rattlesnake, he gets bitten; and if he stands in the way of a rushing train, he is crushed to death.

The ministry of Jesus was an attempt to get people to turn away from sin because he saw clearly the consequences of sin. He called the ultimate consequence "darkness" and "outer darkness." He made it plain that he understood man's fatal obsession with darkness, and that man is drawn to the darkness not the light. He called himself "Light," and he asked man to turn from facing the darkness to facing the light. He knew that death lay in the darkness and life in the light and that the turning and the facing are deep moral acts of renouncing death and accepting life, renouncing wrong and accepting truth, renouncing the past, and accepting the future.

In speaking to John on Patmos, Jesus linked together three important truths about himself. First he said, "I am

THE HOLY OPTION

the first and the last. I am now, I was at the beginning and I will be in the future" (cf. Rev. 1:8). Then he said, "I died and I am alive" (cf. Rev. 1:18) and finally, "I have the keys of Death and Hades" (Rev. 1:18, RSV). He placed himself on both sides of the lives of men, the before and the after. He also placed himself squarely in the lives of men, in the now. He holds the secret to the ghost that troubles man most of all—death. This is profound truth; and if man lets himself think about it for a while, he will become greatly troubled.

Why is this true? Why does a man fall under deep conviction when he begins to think about his sin and its inevitable payoff, the death of the soul? Why? Because the Holy Spirit speaks to him in a direct and intimate way. He speaks not only of the sin but of its remedy. He speaks of the Son of God standing there before him, the first and the last, the now, as dead but alive with the keys of death and hell. The Holy Spirit makes him aware of the horror of the darkness of death by showing him the incomparable Light of life.

You have ignored the only way out. No matter what sin one talks about, he comes finally to the greatest sin of all, rejecting Jesus Christ. Jesus put it plainly, "They are wrong about sin, because they do not believe in me."

This is a mystery that sets before every man a sharp irrevocable life option: to believe in Jesus is to be saved from sin, to have one's sin forgiven; and not to believe in him is to continue in sin, and to perish forever in sin. The gentle loving John, whose philosophical insights rank with those of the lofty Paul, saw this option as pivotal in Christian thought, as one of the great inescapables of the gospel, and as the crux of the issue of life and death. He recorded from Jesus: "He who believes in him is not condemned: he who does not believe is condemned already, because he has not believed in the name of the only Son of God" (John 3:18, RSV).

The doctor in his laboratory looks through his microscope at the tiny specimen of the black wart and calls it "cancer." He turns to the patient and says, "You are under judgment and I am here to help you. You have the cancer because you have not gotten rid of it. If you do what I say, you will live. If you do not do what I say, you will surely die. What is your choice?" The doctor does not condemn the man, the disease condemns him. Jesus does not condemn the sinner, but the sinner's sin does condemn him. In fact, the sinner is already condemned by his sin, just as the man is already condemned by his disease.

Jesus stands before man with the holy option in hand. He offers life, eternal life, and not to take it is death. This then makes unbelief in Christ the great reigning sin, the great ruining sin, and at the bottom of all sin. Apart from Christ there is no righteousness. God is not offering a bandage for a bleeding birthmark, but his own blood for man's soul sickness. He is not playing a child's game, but confronting man with a man's choice. Live or die, the option is yours.

But let us not forget the point of the setting of the text. It is this: the Holy Spirit convicts us of the truth of this great choice in Christ. He tells us Christ is real. Natural law teaches us not to lie, or to steal, or to kill but only the Holy Spirit of God in man teaches us that there is truth and life in Christ. The work of the Spirit is to "convict" or "convince," that is, to "prove" the world wrong about sin. There is no way for a man to arrive at the conviction that his sin is terribly and deeply wrong except

THE HOLY OPTION

that the Spirit awaken him, and no way for him to see Christ as his Savior except the Spirit open his heart.

Cold comfort this is, some will say, yet there it is—God's truth, hard words, "And when he comes he will prove to the people of the world that they are wrong about sin . . . because they do not believe in me" (John 16:8-9, TEV). Be assured of the reality of these words by another hard saying of Jesus: "Everyone who hears these words of mine and does not obey them will be like a foolish man who built his house on the sand" (Matt. 7:26, TEV).

12

The Firebringer

> "I came to set the earth on fire, and how I wish it were already kindled" (Luke 12:49, TEV).

"Fire" is a word for which there are no satisfactory synonyms. "Conflagration" is clumsy and affected; and "scintilla" which barely denotes fire is meaningless to most people. Even the dictionary must define it in chemical terms: exothermic combination of a combustible substance with oxygen. Yet "fire" is "fire," as even children know, especially when it is experienced literally. But when it is experienced symbolically, its meaning is as elusive as its flames. It is a hard stubborn word. This makes the fire text of Jesus difficult to understand, but fascinating to study.

When he said, "I came to set the earth on fire," he spoke a riddle of profound truth, one that testifies to the radical and mysterious nature of Christ's mission. If you take him literally, the saying refers to the end of time when "the elements will be dissolved with fire" (2 Pet. 3:10, RSV), but this idea, not often advanced, does not fit the context. Some have called the fire "the word of God," and others have called it "love." A few have called it "the preaching of the gospel."

One of the oldest and most common interpretations is that the fire is "the Holy Spirit," a completely plausible explanation, in the light of the pentecostal appearance of "tongues as of fire, distributed and resting on each one of them" (Acts 2:3, RSV). This view was held by Alexander Maclaren: "It is God's divine Spirit which Christ came to communicate to the world." He defended his position: "It is not merely a quickened intelligence, a higher moral life, or any other of the spiritual and religious transformations which are effected in the world by the mission of Christ . . . but it is the Heavensent cause of these transformations and that flame." [1]

The most common and difficult interpretation reflects the few verses that follow the text: "Do you suppose that I came to bring peace to the world? Not peace, I tell you, but division. From now on a family of five will be divided, three against two, two against three. Fathers will be against their sons, and sons against their fathers." (Luke 12:51-53, TEV). "Fire" used like this means a revolutionary disturbance. People find this very hard to accept.

Most people do not want to believe that when the gospel is introduced into the world that it brings persecutions, afflictions, dissentions, and strifes. They would like to forget that "fire" is used in the Old Testament as a sign of trouble and affliction. Yet the psalmist said, "Thou didst lay affliction on our loins. . . . We went through fire" (Ps. 66:11-12, RSV). And God said through Hosea, "I will send a fire upon his cities" (Hos. 8:14, RSV). Like so many other biblical sayings, the truth of it is written daily in human experience.

As if interpreting his own fire text, Jesus said, "Not peace, but division." Fathers against sons, mothers against daughters. Yes, the world will always be divided over him. But how can he be healer and disturber at the same time? How can he be simultaneously peacemaker and firebringer? The world finds it hard to accept this dual role for Christ, and even if they accept it in him, they find it even more difficult to follow him in it. A fierce enthusiasm born of the Spirit of God in the hearts of believers creates an equally fierce antagonism in the hearts of unbelievers.

There is truth in all of these interpretations, and they are all conditioned by the others. Whatever else the fire is, if you look at it carefully you will see that it is love, it is the preaching of the gospel, it is the Holy Spirit, it is conflict in the world, and the consummation of all things. Fire is all this and more, for it is the Word of God spoken from the heart of God to man. In short, it is Christ himself as the great triumphant glow of God to the dark night of the heart of man, God's great communication to the world.

Two other sayings of Jesus make it even harder. The healing Christ speaks to man in a most disturbing manner.

Some Christians find this dual role of Christ difficult to understand; and many of them, not really accepting the mission of Christ to the world ignore its demands upon them, go sweetly on their ways, and never confront others with the real gospel. They refuse to become firebrands for the Firebringer, much preferring to be candles under a basket, not torches on a hill.

He warned his disciples, "I have not come to bring peace, but a sword" (Matt. 10:34, RSV). He did not mean by this that his kingdom was one of worldly warfare with troops clashing and men killing one another, but he did mean war, not just of words either, but of deeds in which men and women become so filled with his fire that they clearly show the world the difference between right and wrong and between the holy and the unholy. His is a flaming sword of fire that divides asunder. It separates families and divides communities because his is indeed a warfare for righteousness.

He said also, "If the world hates you, you must remember that it has hated me first. . . . They would not have been guilty of sin if I had not come and spoken to them; as it is, they no longer have any excuse for their sin" (John 15:18,22, TEV). Jesus has brought the evidence that the world is sinful, and that it stands guilty and condemned. So following an instinct as old as mankind, the world fights the witness with hatred. The dividing asunder goes on and the mandate to his followers is plain indeed. He confronts them with chilling fire: "So the world does not hate you? Indeed how could it hate you? Your fire is cold. It does not burn. You don't stand for right. How could the world hate anyone so spineless for right?"

Jesus said of the fire, "How I wish it were already kindled." Karl Barth said that even yet it has not been kindled. Smoke everywhere, but the fire does not burn as God intended it to burn. What goes into fire is always changed, and the world is not really changed. There is far too much sin and suffering, and Christians are so little concerned. They warm themselves in the glow but they don't always let it break out into a fire that warms others. The lower lights are not really burning, at least not for most of the world's hungry and suffering.

Jesus makes clear that his kingdom is a fierce driving action, a spreading fire that cannot be quenched. It is his life that is in the flames, and it is his glow that kindles other lives, even to the point of dividing families and nations. Our darkness and our inaction will not extinguish that fire. If we fall the victims of our own coldness, other hearts will be ignited and the fire will burn on and on.

The burning gospel is a restless gospel and will not be content to smoulder behind church walls or inside timid hearts. It must burn in the streets, in the centers of power, in the political counsels, in the marketplaces, and in the halls of learning. And wherever it burns, it will be a dividing asunder. This is a hard truth, but that is the way it is. It awaits faith and courage, for the fire burns for the weak and the powerless, but never for the timid and the afraid.

13
The Hardest Truth

> "For to every one who has, even more will be given, and he will have more than enough; but the one who has nothing, even the little he has will be taken away from him" (Matt. 25:29, TEV).

M. Theron Rankin once called this the hardest saying in the New Testament. He pondered it as a young missionary in China when he saw hordes of starving Chinese living in hovels around the splendid palaces of their rulers. He thought about it as a prisoner of war when he saw some Christians grow stronger through their sufferings and some deteriorate in character and conscience. He thought about it as he saw America grow richer in the post-World War II days while the have-not nations continued to starve. He continued to think about it up to the end of his life, accepting it as true, yet not knowing why or how it was true, and feeling with deep conviction that in the midst of its naked, harsh reality Jesus Christ stood as an explanation of its enigma.

The writers of the Synoptic Gospels were apparently puzzled by it. They perhaps heard Jesus speak it many times. Matthew picked it up as a side reference on the secrets of the kingdom in connection with the parable of the sower and as one of the main points of the parable of the talents. Mark and Luke used it with the parable of the lamp under a bowl. Mark and Luke relate it to hearing or listening, and Luke alone added the words, "the little he thinks he has" (Luke 8:18, TEV).

The scholars are as puzzled by the text as Dr. Rankin. One calls it "hard but inexorable." Others, "paradoxical but true," "a cynical proverb," and "unknowable." A few of them believe it applies only to grace as it comes to man, but most think it applies to all of life. Most think it is a universal law.

Writers who believe that it applies to everything literally mean it: thoughts, faith, responsibility, trust, effort, skill, talent, spiritual responsibility, material possessions, and countless other things. Thus, the more one thinks, the better he understands; the less he thinks, the less he understands; and the more money he has, the more he will get; and having little or none, he gets even less. The applications are endless in conjecture, and endless in life.

Thinking about it, one knows the saying is true: a man with many talents goes on to unfold those talents to more and more uses, until his whole life is one long succession of opportunities and honors. Another with only one talent buries it and years later digs it up to find it cankered and spoiled. One man with money keeps banking it until he owns the bank, and another keeps losing the little he has until the bank owns him. Surely some who read these words will say, "Yes. This has been the story of my life."

We know that in these words Jesus spoke the truth, yet we don't know precisely why they are true, or how they are true. If we do not believe him, we call the saying "a cynical proverb," and if we do believe in him, we call it "hard but inexorable" or "life's great inequality." There does seem to be an inevitability about the movement of life, we either seem to be moving from better to worse, or from worse to better. Tragedies and triumphs, some have observed, come by threes and fours.

The reward of one success is another. Nothing succeeds like success is a truism embedded deep in the Western mind, and not surprisingly, the New Testament seems to agree with it. In the parable of the talents the Master told his enterprising servant, "You have been faithful over little, I will set you over much" (Matt. 25:23, RSV).

One man gets dozens of job opportunities without asking, another gets none even after constant pleading. One youth gets honors in high school, and even more in college, while another comes to his commencement with scarcely an honor to lift him up for life. Yet both are of equal ability and talent. Why is it this way? This is a stubborn question, but there it is as plain as life. The reward of one success is another. "The soul of the diligent shall be made fat" (Prov. 13:4). The other side of the paradox is also true.

The reward of one failure is another. One of the Proverbs warns us, "an idle soul shall suffer hunger" (Prov. 19:15). A bright child with a bubbling open enthusiasm for life goes happily to his first year of school, but somehow he does not learn what it means to learn. He is given ten words to spell, and learns only five; the next week he is given ten more and again learns only five. This means he now does not know ten words he should know. But the next week, he is given ten more, and again he learns only five.

Failure mounts higher and higher. The teacher rewards the boy who learned the ten and shamed the boy who learned only five. The child deeply condemns himself, and gradually gets into the habit of seeing himself a failure. He forms a picture of himself as a loser, and he takes with himself this negative self-image into all of life's situations. He becomes a procrastinator and an idler because he begins to feel that whatever he touches will surely fail. Outside he is tough and hard and even cocky. Inside he is a cringing, defeated, and self-despising human being. Sadly, the reward of one failure is indeed another failure.

Consider now two human beings, one is a winner and the other is a loser. Jesus Christ addresses both of them from inside this tough hard word. Luke uses the terms "the little he thinks he has." This could be applied to both sides of the paradox. The victories of the winners and the failures of the losers may both be the illusions of life. Whether they are or not, Jesus Christ stands confronting both the winners and the losers, and he wants them to see that he is the real difference in life success and life failure. Without him success is an illusion, with him failure is an illusion. Without him the winners are losers, but with him the losers are winners.

The winners in life are too often the proud and the boastful. You've heard the overtones of pride even in ministers like the one who said, "If I had not been a minister, my talents are such that I could have been a millionaire." The man counts his blessings and credits himself. He defies anybody to rob him of his talent. In contrast with him, the loser in life is a gut-eater. He moans, "It might have been," "I almost made it," "The next time I will," and he waits for a miracle to happen.

Both men are right, and both are wrong. The winner is right in loving himself, or as we might say another way in having a good self-image. He is wrong in crediting himself with that image. The loser is wrong in clinging forever to his poor self-image and so wrong in chewing himself to pieces with remorse and self-depreciation.

The loser is right in expecting a miracle, for it was to

THE HARDEST TRUTH

make a miracle in the life of man that Jesus offered himself, but of course it was for a miracle different from that which the loser looks for. He expects a miracle that will turn his failings into succeedings. Jesus offers a miracle that will turn *him* from a failure into success.

The Gospel writers did not use the word "hear" without purpose. The hardest thing Jesus had to do was to get man really to listen to what he said. He once quoted Isaiah's passage about ears heavy, eyes closed, hearts dull, and asked that his listeners, "Understand *with their heart, and turn for me to heal them*" (Matt. 13:15, RSV). He also said, "For there is nothing hid, except to be made manifest; nor is anything secret, except to come to light" (Mark 4:22, RSV).

Hearing and openness are essential gospel concepts. Success begins the moment a man really makes peace with God concerning the manner of man he now is and is to become. To do this he must (1) listen or hear what God is saying to him about himself, (2) put everything about himself out in the open where it can be seen, and (3) take whatever it is that God has given him to become and work it with all his heart and soul.

No more pride, no more gut chewing, no more measuring one's own light by the light of others, no more guilt, no more scruples, no more fear of the future, no more rotten self-images, no more soul sickness—all these things from God—this is the way that brings the true miracle into the life of a man and turns him suddenly from a have-not and a being-not to a having and a being.

So then the real point of these words so hard and so inexorable is not merely that they are true, but that through Jesus Christ the power of God can come to any man who is caught in their cynical and paradoxical trap. Jesus offers to every man an escape from what seems to be an inevitable life trap, not by changing the trap, but by changing him. And with that change will come a new understanding of the meaning of the gifts of God. He will see that they are not given like Christmas gifts, but like green plants which need an adequate soil for their growth. That's it, the miracle of the new being is that God makes out of us a suitable soil for his own winning through us.

14
The Making of a Fool

"Whoever calls his brother a worthless fool shall be in danger of going to the hell of fire" (Matt. 5:22, TEV).

Are you a name caller? Do you put labels on other people? Do you let them make you angry? Do you call them fools? Do you sneer at them, spit on them, as it were?

And as you hear these questions, do you become defensive and say to yourself, "How can I be honest and not name a man for what he is? To judge others is my right." You may even add, "The whole world is doing it."

Yes, the whole world indeed is doing it, and Jesus taught that it is terribly wrong. He said, "I say to you that every one who is angry with his brother shall be liable to judgment; whoever insults his brother shall be liable to the council, and whoever says, 'You fool!' shall be liable to the hell of fire" (Matt. 5:22, RSV).

These words are hard to believe, for we do not want to give up what we believe is our right to put others in their places. We stubbornly cling to our habits of being angry with others without cause and of condemning them if we choose. We don't realize that Jesus was millennia ahead of modern behaviorists and that he was saying, "Your anger brings *you* under suspicion, your scorn labels *you*, and your condemnation condemns *you*." The simple truth is that one who destroys others also destroys himself.

It is an easy downward path to follow: from anger to scorn to condemnation, and it leads into an incredible personal darkness: from suspicion to ostracism to destruction. When one calls another a fool, he is really making a fool of himself. He is breaking both of the great commandments. He is not honoring God, and he is not loving his neighbor.

To call another person a fool is to dishonor God. In fact, it is to win out in your personal warfare against God and to put him to death in your own soul. In condemning others you are stealing the throne of God. Did he not say, "Vengeance is mine, I will repay" (Rom. 12:19, RSV)? In this he meant, "If there is judgment to make, I will make it, and if there is punishment to give, I will give it."

Such truth is too much for most men. They are determined to sit as lawmakers and as prosecutors, as judges and juries, and as jailers and executioners of other people. They are the people haters, the people scorners, and the name callers. All they know is the rule of self.

Are you one of these? Have you stolen the throne of God and do you sit upon it making a god out of yourself, destroying other people, putting them down in order to build up your own ego? Is your daily conversation one long series of judgmentalisms?

No wonder Jesus said that it is you who is under suspicion, and who is being shut out, and who is stumbling toward condemnation. If you win in your war of words against others, it will mean that you will finally banish God completely from your life and will yourself become a complete fool. The psalmist said that the ultimate fool is one who has said in his heart, "There is no God" (Ps. 14:1, RSV).

THE MAKING OF A FOOL

To call another man a fool is to hate yourself. Among the other hard sayings of Jesus are the words, "Not what goes into the mouth defiles a man, but what comes out of the mouth, this defiles a man" (Matt. 15:10, RSV), and "For out of the mouth come evil thoughts, murder, adultery, fornication, theft, false witness, slander" (Matt. 15:19, RSV). Notice especially the word "slander" which can also be translated as "blasphemies," "railings," or "profane speaking."

Hate talk tells more about the hater than the hated. We don't seem to be able to get it into our heads that the labels we pin on other people are merely labels we have torn out of our own hearts.

Once in a small group led by a behavioral scientist, we were told to go to our rooms and think of all the evil things we could say about a person we did not like, and then stand before a mirror and repeat these things over and over and then come back and tell the group our feelings. Many of those reporting said that they discovered for the first time the weaknesses they saw in others were really only projections of their own shortcomings. If one was secretly angry, he accused others of anger; if overbearing, he accused others of being overbearing. This is not an invariable rule, but it is universally recognizable in all people some of the time.

The behavioral scientist seemed to think that it was a new discovery. Actually Jesus long ago understood this, and he taught that one man calls another man a fool because he himself is a fool. Judas who clutched the money bag tightly in his hands was the first to deny his guilt of betrayal.

Men almost universally defend themselves by attacking others. The blackest heart of all calls the other person a hypocrite. A sick man sees poor color in the faces of other people, reflecting his own sickness. Sometimes one accuses others of moral sickness out of an inner self-hatred. Perhaps if we get over ourselves being fools, we won't call others "fools."

The words "Love thy self" are as much a part of the second command as "Love thy neighbor." The people with the poorest interpersonal relationships are often those who don't really like themselves. They carry guilt about themselves, either real or imagined. They perhaps even regard themselves as fools.

So you don't want to be a fool? Well then, you must accept the reality of this saying of Jesus. You will approach your brothers, not with exclamation marks, but with colon marks. You will always be open with them. Imperatives and exclamations destroy openness and prejudge the facts; colon marks promote openness and reality.

Jesus does not mean for sin to go unpunished, but he does want it truly understood who is the sinner. He does not mean for judgments not to be made, but he wants them to be made in an atmosphere of freedom and understanding.

Maybe it would help if we truly made room for God in our hearts.

15
Knowing God

"No one knows who the Father is except the Son and those to whom the Son wants to reveal him" (Luke 10:22, TEV).

These twenty words stop men still in their thoughts, like a first view of the Grand Canyon or the Niagara Falls. They open a panorama breathtaking and mysterious. The believer looks in awe and faith, the unbeliever in doubt and confusion.

When one studies them, he studies not merely the words, but the whole message of the Bible. It is not the text he is trying to understand, but the lofty concept of God's revelation of himself in Christ.

One deals here with man's knowledge of God—how he knows, what he knows, and from whom he knows. "Epistemology," the theologians call it, but you can forget that big word and try to confirm the truth of the text in your own experience.

The unbeliever sees four things hard for him to understand: (1) that God is knowable, (2) that Jesus knows him, (3) that Jesus gives this knowledge to others, and (4) that he gives it to whom he will.

There is enough in this claim to shake the thinking man, especially if he is the type to demand proof. Those who know only as the world knows often stand dumb, wondering what others see who claim to see the truth in it. They begin by saying that God cannot be known.

The text, of course, refutes them.

God is knowable. He is not easily known or quickly known and the man who thinks he has discovered God on his own is the one least likely to know him. Zophar, the Naamathite challenged Job, "Canst thou by searching find out God? canst thou find out the Almighty unto perfection?" (Job 11:7). Elihu said, "Touching the Almighty, we cannot find him out" (Job 37:23).

Some have accepted him as an interesting idea but completely out of reach of man. Matthew Arnold said of him, "A term thrown out . . . not fully grasped." [1] Others have made war against him. Nietzsche said that the invention of God was "the blunder of man . . . one of the most corrupt concepts that has ever been set up in the world."

Jesus said that he is knowable and that he knew him. The believer knows that his claims are true. He knows it is fair to ask, "How do you know that he can know?"

Literally, hundreds of thousands of pages have been written in answer to that question. Many profound and significant things have been said, yet all of them taken together do not fully satisfy. For those looking for proof as the world demands proof, the answers do not convince.

One of the early church fathers pointed to the difficulty saying, "God is not the name of God, but an opinion about him." St. Augustine said, "God is best known in not knowing him." Richard Hooker said, "Our soundest knowledge is to know that we know him not as indeed he is, neither can know him; and our eloquence concerning him is our silence." Yet, these men did know God as Jesus knew him and revealed him. Their proof for him was not in facts or in words but in their own hearts.

Jesus knew God. Here again the vastness of his claim only adds to its incredibility for man. Nevertheless, it is the claim of faith that he knew God. John said of him, "In the beginning was the Word, and the Word was with God, and the Word was God. He was in the beginning with God; all things were made through him, and without him was not anything made that was made" (John 1:1-3, RSV).

For John, Jesus was the Word of God and the Son of God, which in a way is like saying that he was God. He based his conviction on some of the things he heard Jesus say, for example on the claim "I and the Father are one" (John 10:30, RSV). Yet John did not come right out and say, "Jesus is God." However, he did say "the Word was God," so you have no doubt but that he meant it, he just didn't directly say, "Jesus is God."

One reason may have been that the humanity of Jesus got in his way. John naturally knew more about Jesus as man than he knew about Jesus as God. He knew him hungry and tired, assaulted and mistreated, and as hurt and dying, and at last he knew him as dead. All of these things marked Jesus as truly a man. Yet afterwards John saw him raised from the dead. John's conclusion had to be that Jesus Christ was very much man and at the same time very much God.

The remarkable hymn with which John opened his gospel story is a testimony of both the divinity and the humanity of Jesus. First the Word with God, then the Word was God, and then "the Word became flesh" (John 1:14, RSV).

John then cried out in his hymn that Moses showed us the law and Jesus Christ showed us God. "No one has ever seen God; the only Son, who is in the bosom of the Father, he has made him known" (John 1:18, RSV).

This is the testimony of faith, and its proof comes in quite a different way than from evidence such as the world supplies. For the moment, this keys the question. To help clear it up, we should look at the next imponderable of this great text.

Jesus gives the knowledge of God to others. Yes, Jesus is the final proof that man can indeed know God, not by climbing a ladder to find him, or by looking into the sunset, or swimming the depths of the sea, or flying into the blue skies. These are fine things to do, but as exalted as our feelings are at such times, they don't really show us God. We just don't find him at the end of a series of logical arguments. Anselm proved that long ago.

How then is knowledge of him mediated through Christ to man? Here again let John speak of what he witnessed. When the Word became flesh, that is when the truly divine became truly man. John said, "We have beheld his glory, glory as of the only Son from the Father . . . and from his fulness have we all received, grace upon grace" (John 1:14,16, RSV). When Jesus appeared, God appeared in him.

Hallelujah, John is saying, we saw the light.

But where is the proof? Not in logic, not in hard human evidence, not in anything that would stand up in a court of law or a scientific laboratory; nevertheless, John said, "We saw the light."

He put it like this, "In him was life, and the life was the light of men" (John 1:4, RSV). We saw him full of grace and glory—we saw God. The revelation of God to the believer comes from Jesus Christ. As he is sought and understood and experienced, he becomes the proof of God. "In him was life, and the life was the light of men" (John 1:4, RSV). God's kingdom is a spiritual kingdom, and knowing it is a spiritual experience. "It is the Spirit that gives light, the flesh is of no avail" (John 6:63, RSV). John experienced Christ as the proof of God.

How does one prove the sun to a blind man? How does he explain it to him? How does he define it? Mere words fall until the blind man is warmed by the sun. So it is with the believer: he knows the Father's love because Jesus has led him into his loving presence.

Yet the unbeliever challenges us, "If you have seen the light, then why have I not seen the light?"

Jesus gives knowledge of God to whom he will. Jesus came to the earth to establish a very special kind of fellowship, a fellowship of loving believers. He does not stand at the end of our questioning or our thinking but at the end of our believing. He rewards faith but not doubt. He opens the eyes only of those who earnestly want their eyes opened as we know from the words, "If any man's will is to do his will, he shall know" (John 7:17, RSV). If through faith we see the Son, we receive the promise for "Every one who sees the Son and believes in him . . . I will raise him up" (John 6:40, RSV).

This is how St. Augustine came to God in the midst of a life of prodigality and how C. S. Lewis found him at the end of a bus trip to a zoo. It is how B. H. Carroll found him while sitting all night in his mother's kitchen after a long bitter experience with atheism. All these men cried out, "We see Jesus," and to them came the great experience of knowing.

Not long ago a middle-aged man came forward at the end of a service. He said that he had been baptized at age sixteen but that it meant nothing. His life was lived in rebellion and growing despair. Finally, he came to the end of his seeking and found Jesus Christ to be what the

Bible says he is, the Savior of man, the mediator between God and man, the revelation of God. At the end of his seeking came believing and turning, and at the end of his believing and turning came knowing.

"What proof is all this?" the unbeliever asks. None, absolutely none, as long as he remains an unbeliever. "You talk riddles and confusion," he says. Yes, "riddles"; but at the beginning we said that is the way it is with unbelievers. Only faith can solve the riddle.

Meanwhile, men of faith marvel at the promise of Jesus. "Many prophets and kings, I tell you, wanted to see what you see, but they could not, and to hear what you hear, but they did not" (Luke 10:24, TEV).

16
"I Call You Friends"

> "I do not call you servants any longer, because a servant does not know what his master is doing. Instead, I call you friends, because I have told you everything I heard from my Father" (John 15:15, TEV).

The prevailing world view of God is that he is a myth. Some say that he is reality, yet they live as if he were an enemy. Others say that he is not an enemy but that he is not concerned with man. And others reason: God is not, but if indeed he is, then he is transcendent and unknowable. To help put down all of this Jesus spoke the simple words, "I call you friends" (John 15:14, TEV).

Christ's presence in human experience dispels the idea that God is myth, for in him God stands really before man and through him God enters really into the heart of man. The first witnesses held resolutely to this conviction even in the face of persecution and death. They saw and accepted Jesus as the Son into whom God poured all of himself.

John said, "The Word became flesh and dwelt among us, full of grace and of truth; we have beheld his glory, glory as of the only Son from the Father" (John 1:14, RSV). Peter said, "We were eyewitnesses of his majesty" (2 Pet. 1:16, RSV). Paul called him, "the likeness of God" (2 Cor. 4:4, RSV), and one "who fills all in all" (Eph. 1:23, RSV), and in whom "the whole fulness of deity dwells bodily" (Col. 2:9, RSV). The author of the Hebrews said, "He reflects the glory of God and bears the very stamp of his nature" (Heb. 1:3, RSV). He was no myth to these men, most of whom had come reluctantly to accept him.

Many men make God their enemy and have assumed that everything God does and wants is against them. They rebel against the words of the Lord's Prayer, "Our Father, . . . thy will be done." They see themselves as their own gods and refuse to put their wills under the rule of another. For them this is like one god giving way to another god. They cannot surrender their personal autonomy. Their ends are certain ruin, because they are gods without power, or at least with only limited human power.

This stubbornness against God is the universal human predicament which led Paul to label such people as "estranged and hostile" (Col. 1:21, RSV), as "enemies" (Rom. 5:10, RSV), and as "children of wrath" (Eph. 2:3, RSV). Most men feel that God is not their friend, else they would not fight him as they do.

Some who do not fight him, ignore him. They believe that God exists but does not care what happens to man. They may speak his name often and they may sing songs about him; but they don't really believe that he stands in relation to man, or that he finally will bring judgment against man. They simply do not see God as personally touching man or as concerned about him. Plainly they have not seen Jesus, for if they had, they would have understood that God knows and cares and that he is in close touch with man.

Such attitudes make it hard for men to understand and accept the friendship of Jesus. Yet this is the salvation of man—that he makes a friend of God by accepting the friendship of Jesus. To truly accept him is to discover a whole new concept of the glory of man and the glory of God. It is for man to see himself as a special creation of God, and to realize that he is not forever lost in the vast cosmic reaches of matter and spirit. It is for man to realize that he is somebody in the eyes of God, an intimate beloved and belonging somebody.

Why is the word "friends" used to describe so profound a transaction? Partly because it is a warm human word, one which man understands and accepts. Also it is a word of universal meaning, denoting an affectionate and intimate relationship. It is the opposite of the word "servant," and "servant" is precisely what Jesus does not call his followers. "I call you *not* servants" (John 15:15). "Friends" is a word of love and freedom and it suggests trust and nearness. "Servant" can be a word of coercion and condescension and it can suggest spying and distance. "Friends" is a loving word; "servants," a legal word. "Friends"—this is exactly what God wants men to become.

We know why Jesus is our friend. He put it simply. It was because God loves us and wants to become our friend. But do we know how he is our friend? Do we understand that the ways of his friendship are endless?

He knows and loves us. Nothing is hidden from him. John said of Jesus, "He himself knew what was in man" (John 2:25, RSV). Once he said that no sparrow falls without God knowing about it, and that even the hairs of our heads are numbered. This means that there is nothing about our lives he does not know—no secret dreams, no hidden sin, no private habit, no inner thought—yet he loves us. Job cried out, "Does not he see my ways, and number all my steps?" (Job 31:4, RSV). Job knew his love, too. This truly is the mark of a friend—to know all about us, and to love us in spite of our shortcomings.

He bears with us. Jesus is no fair-weather friend. He does not desert us when we are weak and when we fall. If we stumble and fall, he picks us up, and if we wander in the dark, he waits for us in the light. There is an appealing story about a boy born blind whom Jesus healed. When the boy went home, he was chided by his neighbors and deserted by his parents at home, and accused by the teachers in the synagogues. Painfully the boy went alone into the streets to find Jesus, his friend, waiting to help him.

Peter was a slow learner. He could not at first understand the deeper meanings of Christ's sayings and he had a difficult time accepting Christ's discipline. He had an unseemly ambition: he kept wanting an earthly kingdom, he overvoiced his zeal, and in a crisis he lied. Jesus knew all this, but he did not desert him. He not only lifted Peter up out of his moral quagmire, he made an apostle out of him. This is the nature of Jesus, to bear with the most inept and careless. This is truly his creative friendship at work in the hearts of sinners.

He both leads us and follows us. He does not browbeat or shame us, nor does he create impossible standards for us. Rather he moves quietly in our presence until he becomes our standard. He lets us see our shortcomings, and then he shows his confidence toward us. He writes on the ground, as it were, while we contemplate our sins, and then he tells us to go and sin no more.

He stood in the presence of Peter not saying a single condemning word. He simply asked, "Lovest thou me?" When Peter saw his sin and realized his love was greater than his sin he cried out, "Thou knowest Lord, I love thee." Jesus then showed his confidence by saying, "Feed my sheep." Only a real lasting friend would do that. He went all the way, too. He said, "I have called you friends, for all that I have heard from the Father I have made known to you" (John 15:15, RSV). Here is friendship of highest trust.

It is true that he could be scathing in his condemnation of sin, but he never spoke harshly to any man. Even when he told the Pharisees that they were like open graves covered with whitewash he used words and tenses to show that he was a grieved father warning his errant sons. It takes a real friend to chastize with love.

He would not send any person to any place he himself would not go, not even to the grave. He asked his followers to scatter to the end of the earth and said, "Lo, I am with you always" (Matt. 28:20, RSV). He is the "friend who sticks closer than a brother" (Prov. 18:24, RSV), the friend to whom no man need fear losing anything.

He pleads for us. An old lawyer who had lost his strength and whose voice had been reduced to a whisper heard a study of the words, "Him who comes to me I will not cast out" (John 6:37, RSV), and "We have an advocate with the Father" (1 John 2:1, RSV). Later he said to his pastor, "Jesus is the perfect lawyer who will not turn down my case no matter how poor and unworthy I am." He could just as well have said that Jesus was his friend, for that is what he is to all of us, a friend to plead our cases before the King. His adversary speaks of the man side of his nature, something we must not forget, for it is as a man who is a friend of all other men that he stands before God. On the other hand, it is as God that he stands before men as the friend of God. He is a special pleader with the blessing of the Father.

Hear him as he prays, "I am praying for them; I am not praying for the world but for those whom thou hast given me, for they are thine; all mine are thine, and thine are mine . . . I am glorified in them . . . Holy Father, keep them in thy name" (John 17:9-11, RSV). The Father surely thought much of that prayer for long before when Job prayed for his friends the Lord turned and heard him and blessed him.

This pleading goes on and on for Paul tells us that it is Jesus Christ "who is at the right hand of God, who intercedes for us" (Rom. 8:34, RSV).

He shares his home with us. Once long ago my friends turned away from me like falling leaves. They thought I had smallpox. Sitting on the side of a hill in fine misting rain I was too sick to move. Out of the woods came a man and asked for my car keys. He said, "Young man, you are going home with me and stay until you get well." I said, "But I may have the smallpox." He answered, "Yes, I know, but that is a chance we will have to take." That man was my friend, my real friend. He shared his home with me when I was ill and helpless.

Jesus goes much further than that. He has preceded us to what the Bible calls the "long home" (Eccl. 12:5), that is, into death. And before he left he said, "In my father's house are many rooms. . . . I go and prepare a place for you, . . . that where I am you may be also" (John 14:2-3, RSV). It takes an extraordinary friend to keep a promise like that.

He lays down his life for me. The ultimate friendship is the one that is proved by death. Jesus said, "Greater love has no man than this, that a man lay down his life for his friends" (John 15:13, RSV). At age twelve I was drowning in a pool of brackish water. A man still sick from a month's illness in bed rescued me. The exposure was too much for him. He went back to bed, grew worse, and died. That man was my friend, and I've never forgotten him. I hear the stamp of his life in my body, because through his death I live.

Jesus is my friend, too. He gave his life for me, standing between me and the destructive powers of sin and death. These are my mortal enemies, yet he calls my name and tells me not to be afraid and says that they shall no more have dominion over me. Long ago when I realized he had called me friend, I decided to call him friend. It has been a long journey, and in my younger years I did not understand the journey as I do now, and yet even now I don't fully understand it, but this I know: my understanding started when I began calling him "friend."

17
With Everything

"You shall love the Lord your God with all your heart, and with all your soul, and with all your mind, and with all your strength." (Mark 12:30, RSV)

How can one love God? It is difficult to know how to respond with affection to one so vast and so unknown. Yet Jesus said not only to love him but to love him totally. "You must love the Lord your God with all your heart, with all your soul, with all your mind, and with all your strength" (Mark 12:30, TEV). He asked man to wholly submit himself to God, and man has always found that hard to do.

Part of the problem is man's misunderstanding of love. The romantic novelists have led him to believe that love is always affection. Because of this, he goes about in a cloud of sentimentality. Too often he regards love as merely something someone else does for him, and he does not see that in its purest essence it is also the things he does for someone else. He does not understand that love is preference, loyalty, service, affinity, empathy, and abandon. His "love and kisses" mentality blinds him to all of this.

So he slams the doors of his heart and dismisses the call of Jesus as idealistic and impossible. If he is the intellectual type, he says the commandment is illogical and incomprehensible. It is a serious thing he does, this closing of the door on the highest and best. In doing so, he emphasizes his estrangement from God and his bitter rebellion against God.

Man attempts to forget God, yet God never forgets him. "God shows his love for us in that while we were yet sinners Christ died for us" (Rom. 5:8, RSV).

What are the doors man so stubbornly closes against this kind of love? One way to answer is to look deeply into this great saying of Jesus. In it he stressed the unity of God and man. His life's mission was their complete integration. The words "heart," "soul," "mind," and "strength" are not to be understood as the compartmentalization of the human self. God is one and man is one, and the whole man must love the whole God.

The four words are different ways of looking at the same thing. Man is *heart* or feeling, yet not heart without *mind* or knowing. He is *soul* or self, yet not soul without feeling and knowing. He is *strength* or body, yet not without knowing, feeling, and self.

These can be thought of as four qualities or functions of life, and it may be said that there is no true authenticity for the human personality without a complete integration of the four. It further may be said that true salvation is not only the integration of the four, but also the integration of the one into God. "Love the Lord your God with *all*."

Even though heart, soul, mind, and strength may be regarded as one, it is useful to look at each one of them as ways of viewing the whole. In doing this, we may be able to see them as doors closed against the entrance of God into our lives.

The door of the unyielded mind. This is perhaps the most tightly closed because it is the one of which man is the most conscious. He guards his mind against surrender to any power that would destroy his autonomy. He wants to do his own remembering, thinking, knowing, anticipating, accepting, and rejecting. He believes that the only way he can survive is to keep others from stealing his freedom. Because God seems to destroy his autonomy, man stubbornly closes his mind to the idea of the reality of God. He does not realize that Christ in him is not the destruction of his right to think. Christ does not destroy minds. Remember he said, "I am life." He enters to reinforce individual uniqueness, not to efface it. He becomes the energizer of the mind, not its suppressor. Yet, obstinately, man holds out against him, refusing to claim the fullness of the true mind that is possible in Christ.

Scientists say that only a portion of a single human mind is ever used. The barrier that stands in the way of its fullest use is man's pride and ego, his unwillingness to let God possess his total consciousness. In his stubbornness, man clings to a shadow of the mind he might have had. He misses the experience of highest fulfillment by never saying, "Lord, here is all my mind, use it for your glory."

There is a mystery in the word used for mind in this text. It clearly denotes intellectual activity plus spiritual activity. To put one's mind to the service of God is not to stop thinking. Rather, it is to multiply thinking, to push outward into the spiritual. It is to leap over the silly notion that life is divided into the spiritual and the secular. It is to find paths through problems sustained by God's love and guided by God's insight. It is to become a prophet.

The door of the unsurrendered heart. This is perhaps almost as tightly closed as the door of the unyielded mind. Modern man thinks of heart as the seat of the feelings. With it he loves, he hates, he exults, he despairs, he trusts, he doubts, he enjoys, and he sorrows. He wants to feel what he feels without any kind of inhibition. This is precisely where he makes his worst mistake. He does not understand that Christ in him is a liberation. He rather thinks Christ demands him in order to enslave him and not to set him free. He will not accept the promise, "If the Son makes you free, you will be free indeed" (John 8:36, RSV).

Perhaps total integration of all of life is most difficult because feeling is the hardest thing of all to bring into harmony with the mind and the body and with the self. Feelings just won't stay fixed. Man is up one day and down the next. His feelings are always getting in the way of good judgment and even in the way of efficient performance of his body.

Feelings are often the uncontrollables of life and are where man needs the most help. But he refuses the integrating force of Christ's presence that can bring even his emotions under control. More than anything else, man nurses his feelings, with or without integration, and he wastes away because feelings without spiritual substance offer a thin, watery, lifeless milk.

There are numerous mental and emotional diseases that are psychotic in nature and definitely need the aid of physicians. But most of man's troubled feelings are all of his own making and cannot be cured until he himself is changed. He seeks joy in things that, in the long run, cannot possibly bring him joy. He becomes a slave to his art, his money, his work, and his fame. Unless he is spiritually sustained, these will become bitter chains around his heart. The weight he will feel is his reluctance to merge his feelings into God's eternal optimistic spirit. Teilhard de Chardin was a Jesuit priest who struggled in his early life between a great love for the study of ancient fossils and his love for Christ. Finally, in a great surrender of himself he came to the point where he could say, "The felicity I had sought in iron, I can find now only in Spirit." [1] He found that in his surrender, God also gave him his fossils, but never again were fossils as important as God. This does not always happen, but it happens enough to make us wonder at the words of Jesus: "Seek first his kingdom and his righteousness, and all these things shall be yours as well" (Matt. 6:33, RSV).

The door of the unsurrendered body. This perhaps is the most misunderstood of the four words. When Jesus used the word "strength," he meant physical life and the force of body, yet he did not mean to separate it from the other functions. His emphasis was the whole life, of which strength or body was one part.

Man's body passions are his joy and his comfort. He likes to express his autonomy in unbridled appetites, and he does not realize that the freedom to eat or to drink or to fornicate he so fiercely guards, itself becomes his prison. Freedom is not found where he expects to find it, in his complete surrender to his bodily appetites. It is found in another unexpected place: in the opening of the door of his body to the indwelling Christ.

Many a man, stubborn in his rebellion against Christ, all in the name of personal liberty, has been surprised in the end to find a hilarious freedom in simply yielding his whole physical being to God. Paul said, "Present your bodies as a living sacrifice, holy and acceptable to God, which is your spiritual worship" (Rom. 12:1, RSV).

This is a strange idea even to Christian ears—that a surrendered body is spiritual worship. This is because they do not understand that the ancient Jew (on whose faith the Christian faith rests) understood body and soul and as one, and that Paul in following the Jewish tradition did not make a hard distinction between life in the flesh and life in the spirit. Perhaps Paul would say now that man does not *have* a body, but he *is* a body. He really is one, flesh made alive by spirit, and psychophysically whole.

It is not becoming for a Christian to talk and act as if the body had no meaning, as some have done in the past, wearing hair shirts, sleeping on bare boards, fasting to the point of starvation, eating inadequate food—all in the name of Christian devotion. This is almost as bad as the unbeliever who soaks his liver with alcohol and destroys his brain with narcotics—all in the name of personal freedom. When Paul said, "I pommel my body and subdue it, lest after preaching to others I myself should be disqualified" (1 Cor. 9:27, RSV), he did not mean that he mistreated his body but that he disciplined it. He kept it as strong and useful as possible for God's service. He refused to become either an aesthetic or a libertine. His idea of the sacredness of the body is clear, "Do you not know that you are God's temple and that God's Spirit dwells in you? If any one destroys God's temple, God will destroy him. For God's temple is holy, and that temple you are" (1 Cor. 3:16, RSV). When Jesus said, "all," he meant the body too.

The door of the stubborn self. Of the four words, *soul* is the most unique and most obscure. In the Old Testament it meant breath, and in the New Testament it could mean "life" or "person" or "self." Perhaps it is the summary word for all four of the words in the text, and it means the "I" of the person. It is important to remember that

Jesus acknowledged the self in the words "love thy neighbour as thyself."

There is no way to set the self on a mountain peak and with a spyglass to look at itself as something apart; yet the self does contemplate itself, and as it contemplates it clings to its autonomy and its freedom, denying Christ the right to a presence within it. It believes that Christ destroys its "I-ness," which, of course, is not true at all. He cleanses and sanctifies the "I-ness," but he does not destroy it. He releases it and gives it life, but he does not make it a robot.

In fact, he turns the robot of self into a living creature. C. S. Lewis illustrated this by saying that Christ turns tin soldiers into live soldiers. He takes the dead and gives them life, and prepares them for the great banquet. In a sense, he gives us a wedding garment: his life, his spirit, his presence, and his power, but only if we choose him. The human will is a fearful thing. We still had rather be an obstinate and dead tin soldier than a live Son of God. And sadly, because of obstinacy, "few are chosen."

With some people "loving God" is a childish thing. They talk glibly about "loving the Lord" as if saying it proved it. When God destroyed the Temple, he put on the rubbish pile all ceremonies and lip service. The proof he looks for is not to be found in mere words and certainly not in creedal professions; it is to be found inside the self in faith and action.

He looks for love in the mind and asks, "How much of your thinking and your consciousness do I possess?" He looks for love in the heart and asks, "How much of your loyalty have you given me?" He looks for love in the body and asks, "How much of your strength have you set to work for me by helping others?" He looks for love in the self and asks, "How much of your personal being has been merged into my being?" If you can say, "All, Lord, all," then truly you love God. What is more, you have learned the hard meaning of one of his hardest sayings—that after it is done, it is easy, because he gives you the strength to do it.

18

The Hardest Commandment

"Love your enemies, and pray for those who mistreat you" (Matt. 5:44, TEV).

Absence of love in the world was the constant concern of Jesus. Love for God was his first commandment, and love for neighbor his second, and for him there was hardly a breath between them. Years after he first spoke this truth, John, his beloved disciple wrote that "God is love" (1 John 4:8), and that "This is the message which you have heard from the beginning, that we should love one another" (1 John 3:11, RSV). Love then is at the very center of the Christian idea. Without it we are nothing, with it we are the sons of God.

This leads us to a consideration of some very plain words that Jesus spoke, words that sound strange and empty to most people: "Love your enemies," he said, "and pray for those who mistreat you" (Matt. 5:44, TEV). Here he set out clearly what had long been partially veiled from the eyes of man. Men of the Old Testament often overlooked God's appeal for universal love. They more often heard a cry for vengeance. Even when the appeal for love should have been clearly seen as in the words "You shall not . . . bear any grudge against the sons of your own people, but you shall love your neighbor as yourself" (Lev. 19:18, RSV) they would often add under their breath, "and

THE HARDEST COMMANDMENT

hate your enemies." The idea prevailed among kings and the common people, "Love your friends, despise your enemies." It still prevails in warfare, business, politics, and even religion. Jesus will have none of it, so he says, "Love your enemies." It is indeed a hard commandment.

It becomes harder still when we look at the long passage from which it is taken. Beginning in Matthew 5:21 Jesus sets forth a series of ethical requirements that climax with his words, "Love your enemies." Don't kill, don't even become angry (v. 22). Reconcile yourself to those who hold grudges against you (v. 23). Make peace with your accusers (v. 25). Don't retaliate for wrongdoing (v. 39). Give to your neighbor who steals from you (v. 40). Go willingly with the man who compels you to walk with him (v. 41). Give freely to beggars and borrowers (v. 42), and finally, love your enemies and pray for those who persecute you (v. 44).

Chrysostom called this progression of ideas stairsteps to the "summit of virtue."

> The first step is, not to begin injuring;
> the second, after injury has begun,
>   not to defend yourself against the injurer by like actions;
> the third, not to inflict on the wrongdoer that which one has suffered, but to keep quiet;
> the fourth, even to yield oneself to suffer evil;
> the fifth, to yield even more than he who did the evil wishes;
> the sixth, not to hate him who does this thing;
> the seventh, even to love him;
> the eighth, even to do him good;
> the ninth, even to pray to God for him.[1]

Nine upward steps to complete moral and spiritual responsibility, each far above the one before, and with the highest one of all—loving one's enemies and entreating God on their behalf. The world hotly defies this ladder of Christian virtue—as the Watergate affair so plainly showed—with men and women alike blaspheming anything or anyone who gets in their way, and seeking cruel revenge for even the slightest opposition or disapproval.

Love your enemies, pray for those who mistreat you—a hard way to go. The alternate way of hate and revenge is the way to peril and defeat. Paul wrote, "Never avenge yourself, but leave it to the wrath of God; for it is written, vengeance is mine. I will repay, says the Lord" (Rom. 12:19, RSV). God reserves for himself the right to protect you from your enemies. But do not be fooled, his protection does not always mean their destruction. Sometimes it means a simple thing like setting a table before you in the presence of your enemies. So compelling is his love that even the dark cloud of God's wrath has love and grace for its silver lining.

When Jesus tells us to love our enemies, he is asking us to participate in his own special kind of love, that which he lavished on the ugliest and most undeserving of people. His call is to come to perfect love—*agape* love—love such as he has for all men, love that bridges gaps and overcomes walls, the kind of love that Paul spoke about, "God shows his love for us, in that while we were yet sinners Christ died for us" (Rom. 5:8, RSV). This is the love of unfailing goodwill, the love of unmerited favor, love that is given in return for hate, love that works for the good of others.

Such love is different from imperfect love—*eros* love, love for self, love that rewards itself. Either we die in imperfect love, or we live in perfect love. In imperfect love are the seeds of death; in perfect love, the seeds of life. It is for this reason that the call of God's kind of

THE HARDEST COMMANDMENT

love is the most radical man will ever face. It is the call for man to turn away from *eros* love which seeks one's own good, to *agape* love which seeks good for others. This perfect love, which the Christian must always be seeking, has many expressions, the ultimate one being, "Love your enemies."

Within the hearts of most men hate and love are strangely mixed. Sometimes men hate and love in the same breath, and sometimes they hate and love the same person. Jesus Christ confronts man, whether he realizes it or not, and calls for a great cleavage of the hate and love in his life. He wants us to tear our hearts in two and throw away the worst part, and to "live purer with the other half." [2] The man who gives way to hatred is hopelessly and ultimately lost, the man who gives way to God's kind of love is victoriously and finally saved.

Where are we on the steps of Chrysostom's lofty ladder of moral perfection?

Painfully, most people have gone no further than doing no harm to their neighbors. Their love is far from perfect, yet perfection is what Jesus finally requires, because four sentences after he asked us to "love our enemies," he said, "You, therefore, must be perfect, as your heavenly father is perfect" (Matt. 5:48, RSV). We must find our perfection in love and in God, and the last step is to do as he did, to love our enemies, and to pray for them.

Arriving is to find spirit and wholeness and to obey the hardest commandment—and to stand at the "summit of virtue."

19

Becoming Perfect

> "You, therefore, must be perfect, as your heavenly Father is perfect" (Matt. 5:48, RSV).

Who is the successful Christian? When has he arrived at perfection of his faith? He who would answer these questions, let him enter his bedroom, look into his mirror, and gaze deeply into his own eyes. If he says, "I am really succeeding," he actually may be faltering. If he says, "I'm not doing as well as I should," he then may be doing very well indeed. The moment one begins to take haughty pride in his Christian accomplishments that very moment he begins to lose his Christian spirit.

The best proof of this is the story Jesus told of two men who prayed in the Temple. The Pharisee stood in a prominent place, proudly raised his hands, and told the Lord that he was grateful that he did everything right and that he was not like the sinners all around him. The publican stood in the corner, beat his chest, and asked the Lord to be merciful to him, a sinner. Jesus made it clear that it was the publican who was truly justified. It is obvious that our Lord expected all men to admit themselves as sinners.

Over against this are the simple words of Jesus, "You . . . must be perfect" (Matt. 5:48, RSV). It is also written of "the holiness without which no one will see the Lord"

(Heb. 12:14, RSV) and that we are to be "perfect and complete, lacking in nothing" (Jas. 1:4). Thus the problem is raised, for on the one hand it is clear that Jesus did not think man could be perfect, and on the other, he demanded perfection and holiness. Surely he meant what he said in both instances.

Some have tried to weaken the word "perfect" by making it apply only to love. Certainly, love is the context of this saying and it must be related to the commandment only four sentences back, "Love your enemies." Yet as John A. Broadus said, "In all things, love included, we ought to be perfect."[1] Most careful students believe that the words are applicable to the whole of the Christian life.

Others have tried to explain the word "perfect" away by making it mean "perfect" in a kind of an imperfect way. For example, a plant is perfect if it is mature. Whether it has all leaves or not is immaterial, it has reached perfection if only it runs its course. There may be truth in this explanation, but it hardly satisfies the idealism of the New Testament.

In pleas for perfection, Jesus is forcing us to look at the Christian life and the way we live it. He wants us to see that there is a right way and a wrong way to judge our success as Christians.

The wrong way to judge Christian success. Some standards appear plausible but will not stand examination.

One is by the amount of bad left undone. Take as an example the rich young ruler who wanted to know the way into the kingdom of God. Jesus told him to keep the commandments. He then said all of them he had kept from childhood and asked, "What lack I yet?" He had explicitly obeyed the law, yet he recognized an inner imperfection. He had left undone all the bad yet had fallen far short of the standards that Jesus set for his disciples. John summed it up, "If we say that we have no sin, we deceive ourselves, and the truth is not in us" (1 John 1:8).

The second wrong way to judge the Christian life is by the amount of good accomplished. This points to man's biggest failure in understanding. He believes it is based on his personal goodness. He measures it by how many good things he can do for others, especially for his friends and loved ones. Surely this is part of it, but only part of it. You might say that doing good is a fringe benefit of the Christian life, recognizing that it is always possible for one to have all the fringe benefits without the essential salary, so to speak. As necessary as good works are, they are not the inner essence of the Christian life. One may do many excellent good things from entirely false motives.

We also must ask the question, "How much or how many good works?" It could be that what is "much" for you is not "much" for me. Anyway Paul said that the Christian life "is the gift of God: not of works, lest any man should boast" (Eph. 2:8-9).

The third wrong way is by the standard of perfection. We are back again in what appears to be direct conflict with the text "You . . . must be perfect." Yet as we have seen, other New Testament teaching makes it plain that Christians are not really perfect, even though some people think they are. One of these chided a pastor for exhorting his people to live holy lives and then closing his sermon with a prayer: "O God, be merciful to me a sinner." The critic asked, "How can you a Christian admit sin?" The minister asked him if he ever prayed the Lord's Prayer. "Yes," he said, "often." The minister asked him what the word "trespasses" meant, and the man said, "Sin." The

BECOMING PERFECT

minister had trapped him, "What do you who claim to be perfect, do about the Lord's Prayer?" The man turned away saying, "I don't know." Later he came to the pastor and said that he had decided the Lord didn't intend for him to pray the Lord's Prayer. Not long after making this strange statement, he deserted his wife and ran away with the pianist in his church. The poor man, by claiming perfection, did not recognize sin in his own life. And yet in spite of man's imperfection Jesus said, "You . . . must be perfect."

The right way to judge Christian success. In thinking about this, we come up against a paradox. The Christian way is both easier and harder. It is easier in that God gives his children the power to do what he requires of them. Moreover, as an alternative to the life of sin, the Christian life is infinitely more rewarding. It is harder because of the high standards Christ sets for his followers. He means for his disciples to be truly different and to be more morally responsible than others. He is getting at this, when he says, "You . . . must be perfect."

He starts with the assumption that his followers have truly turned around. They have left their backward looking toward sin and have set their gaze forward toward him. In short, they have been converted, and the essence of their conversion is an experience of faith in the Lord. Christ stands before them and they are moving toward him. There is no Christian life without a beginning.

Jesus also assumes that people are different, a fact he made plain in the parable of the talents. Some have more ability than others, some more endurance, and some more understanding. Also, there are differences in where people start their Christian lives. One man because of training from his childhood may have a better understanding than another less fortunate. One child walks at 10 months, another at 16 months, but in adolescence the late walker may be the fast runner. One child talks at 12 months, another is still tongue-tied at 24 months, yet down the way the second child may become the better talker. Surely, the variety and diversity of life, as well as its tempo, its quality, and its depth raise questions of the need for a special kind of standard for judging the success of the Christian life.

Jesus also assumes that his followers will grow in their spiritual and moral life. He chose twelve simple men as disciples, eleven of them grew, one of them didn't. Among the eleven some grew more than the others. Peter became a leader and a preacher, Luke became a gospel historian, John became a spiritual father, James became a great moralist, and Thomas a devout believer.

The Christian life starts as a "turning around," a willing "facing toward Christ," and a simple step in faith toward him. It is at this point that Jesus says, "You . . . must be perfect." Not today, perhaps, but sometime. He did not expect Peter to be perfect the first day of his new life; he expected him in time to be perfect.

The perfection he offers is ultimate perfection in himself, as he becomes our righteousness. It comes at the end of our spiritual wishing, trying, and hoping. In the Christian walk, "We should *wish* to be perfect—and pained with our imperfections. We should *try* to be perfect—not disheartened by past failures. We may *hope* to be perfect—as we pass into the perfect world." [2] Perfection then is the thing we strive for, and if we are content not to possess it, we should wonder if we are truly sons of God. We

BECOMING PERFECT

must not assume, however, that the wishing, the trying, and the hoping purchase the perfection. They only indicate our willingness to receive it. The fullness of God comes only as the gift of God, and the medium of the gift is Jesus Christ. It is his perfection we receive, and it is his own sanctified nature that he gives to us. In reality, our perfection is Christ in us, God himself enthroning himself in our lives. This is the ultimate test—Christ in us, the Lord and Master of our lives.

Jesus expects every Christian daily to beat his own best record. He does not expect them to measure themselves by what others are able to do but only by what they can do that is an improvement on what they have done before. A spastic adolescent boy came halting and stumbling to the minister and said in a thick, dull voice, "You have helped me, I will try to do better." The minister thought, "What can he do? He can't sing or teach. He can't visit. What?" The next morning he received his answer. On the way to catch a five o'clock bus, he was surprised to see the boy selling papers, and so he bought one. On the bus he unfolded the paper, and inside he found a gospel tract. The boy could do what he could do, and he could do it better than he had done it yesterday. This has marvelous meaning for the Christian. One does not have to teach or pray better than others, only better than he himself has done them before. This gives hope for the weakest Christian and challenge for the strongest. The Lord is pleased with his children when he sees growth from where they are. In this way every Christian is finally "mature in Christ" (Col. 1:28, RSV).

How can we arrive at such perfection? Well, it's not easy, and at times the progress we make seems painfully slow. Before me as I write is a boy twelve years old who says he wants to be a marine biologist. He is bright, gifted, and apparently trying very hard. He reads books, studies French and Spanish, plays the violin, and experiments with models of submersible ships trying to find one he says, "For perfect marine observation." But he has problems as I can plainly see from his fingernails which are chewed to the quick. He has two mothers and three fathers, which he says "is a confusing situation." His sister works in a pizza parlor, and he sometimes helps her he says and slips his tip in her tip box. He is a loner, he admits, but claims to have 20 close friends, and 35 not so close. He weighs 176 pounds and can lift 265 pounds of barbells "if excited."

Down the street lives another boy about the same age, perhaps a little older, but retarded. He cannot carry on a conversation and he repeats his words rote fashion. Each morning he stands at the corner with a shovel in hand, in slow witted imitation of some older man, perhaps his father.

Here we have two human beings vastly separated in ability, understanding, skill, and accomplishment, each far from perfection, and illustrating the Christian walk. One is no more perfect than the other. If we were to say to them, "You must be a man," obviously each would have a long way to go. Their success would be relative. The one given the most would be required to do the most, yet mere doing would not make him a man. The important thing is not that they have already achieved manhood but that they are pressing forward, each in his own way, one in painful imitation of his father, the other by "learning about 15 new things every day." This gives us an idea where we stand in moral and spiritual imperfection. Some are more responsible than others, and some stand higher than others. The important thing for us is that we are pressing forward, wishing, trying, hoping. It is just as Paul said, "Not that I . . . am already perfect; but I press on . . . because Christ Jesus has made me his own" (Phil. 3:12, RSV). The trying, wishing, hoping, are now; the perfecting is yet to come.

Notes

Chapter 1
1. Herschel H. Hobbs, *An Exposition of the Gospel of Matthew* (Grand Rapids: Baker Book House, 1972), 84.
2. *An American Commentary of the New Testament* (New York: American Baptist, 1886) I, 164.
3. *Ellicott's Commentary of the Whole Bible* (Grand Rapids: Zondervan), VI, 42.
4. *Lange's Commentary on the Holy Scriptures* (Grand Rapids: Zondervan), Matthew, 143, col. 2.
5. *Matthew Henry's Commentary* (New York: Fleming H. Revell), V, 92, col. 2.
6. William Barclay, *The Gospel of Matthew* (Philadelphia: The Westminster Press, 1958), I, 282.

Chapter 3
1. Dietrich von Hildebrand, *Transformation in Christ* (New York: Image, 1962), pp. 176 ff.
2. Quoted by Nicolai Berdyaev, *Christian Existentialism* (New York: Harper & Row, 1963), p. 138.
3. *Ibid.*

Chapter 5
1. Expositor's Greek New Testament, Vol. 1, p. 283 (PD).

Chapter 6
1. *Op. cit.*, p. 88.

Chapter 7
1. *Matthew Henry's Commentary*, V, 286.
2. Frank Stagg, *The Broadman Bible Commentary* 8 (Nashville: Broadman Press, 1969), 205.
3. From *The Bible, a New Translation* by James Moffatt.

Chapter 9
1. Lange on Luke, p. 161 (PD).

Chapter 10
1. *Op. cit.*, p. 202.

Chapter 12
1. *Exposition of the Holy Scripture*, Alexander Maclaren, IX, 383.

Chapter 15
1. H. L. Mencken, *A New Dictionary of Quotations* (New York: Knoff, 1946), p. 466.

Chapter 17
1. Teilhard de Chardin, *The Divine Mile* (New York: Harper & Row, 1965), p. 22.

Chapter 18
1. Quoted by John A. Broadus in *Commentary on Matthew*, p. 125.
2. *Hamlet*, III, 4.

Chapter 19
1. *Op. cit.*, p. 124.
2. *Ibid.*, p. 125.